When You Come Unglued ...
Stick Close to God

*June Sackett*

# When You Come Unglued ...
## Stick Close to God

## patricia wilson

UPPER
ROOM BOOKS®
NASHVILLE

Cover image: White Packert / gettyimages.com
Cover design: Bruce deRoos / Left Coast Design
Interior design: Nancy Terzian / Nter Design
First printing: 2007

*Library of Congress Cataloging-in-Publication Data*

Wilson, Patricia, 1943–
    When you come unglued— stick close to God / by Patricia Wilson.
        p. cm.
    ISBN 978-0-8358-9918-5
    1. Spirituality.    2. Spiritual life—Christianity. I. Title.
    BV4501.3.W556 2007
    248.4—dc22                                        2007021007

*In memory of my mother,*
*Pauline Wilson*

# Contents

# Preface

Writing a book is a journey that takes time. From the first glimmering of an idea to the final edit of a manuscript, years may pass. In those intervening years, life continues to be lived. Writing a Christian book presents even more challenge since that lived life usually causes a change in perception and belief, even as the writer puts words on paper.

Since I started this book, four years have passed, and in that period, I've moved three times, attended my son's wedding, rejoiced at the birth of three grandchildren, mourned the deaths of my mother and my uncle, endured two major surgeries, written two secular books, enjoyed success as a motivational speaker, retired from my "road warrior" career, lost and gained twenty pounds more than once, renovated two homes, bought and sold properties, attended funerals of three good friends, moved away from my island home to an urban environment, and watched the world spin out of control. I've come unglued more than once!

If nothing else, the past four years have taught me a little humility. Sticking close to God is not as easy as I thought it would be—not because God moved on to someone less difficult and demanding but because I keep forgetting that my walk with God requires a conscious, daily decision.

That's what this book is all about: how to consciously, daily stick close to God, even on those days and through those times when life comes unglued!

# Introduction

## The Rock of Ages Does Not Move!

At some time in our lives, we who call ourselves Christians made a choice to follow Jesus. Perhaps it was a watershed experience for you—a moment in time that you can pinpoint exactly. That's how it was for me—January 9, 1967. Or perhaps, like many others, you can't remember a time when Jesus wasn't part of your life.

Now you may be finding that your Christian walk has become a little less exciting. The years have gone by, and with each passing day you may feel more and more disconnected from the life promised to you as a consequence of your choice. Where is the joy, the awe, the awareness of God's presence in your life? You may find yourself blaming God for your feelings of emptiness. You may even be angry with God for leaving you to cope with life on your own. Perhaps you feel that your prayers go nowhere, that you're simply praying into a dark vacuum, void of God's presence.

If this is how you feel, you're not alone. Consider the Psalms. Even the psalmist endured the feeling that he was apart from God, separated, alone, deserted.

Why, O LORD, do you stand far off?
  Why do you hide yourself
    in times of trouble? (Psalm 10:1, NIV)

How long, O LORD? Will you forget me forever?
  How long will you hide your face from me?
How long must I wrestle with my thoughts
  and every day have sorrow in my heart?
    (Psalm 13:1-2, NIV)

My God, my God, why have you
    forsaken me?
  Why are you so far from saving me,
    so far from the words of my groaning?
O my God, I cry out by day, but you
    do not answer,
  by night, and am not silent. (Psalm 22:1-2, NIV)

Do not hide your face from me,
  do not turn your servant way in anger;
  you have been my helper.
Do not reject me or forsake me,
  O God my Savior. (Psalm 27:9, NIV)

Sound familiar? The psalmist made the same assumption we all do when we feel God is no longer near to us. We assume God has moved away from us or has banished us from God's presence. In fact, we have allowed ourselves to be slowly, inexorably, pushed out of the glory of God's presence. How does this happen?

In this book, we'll look at some of the feelings, behaviors, and experiences that distance us from God:

- sense of purposelessness and lack of direction in our lives
- burdens of the past and the fears for the future
- demands of others and of the world around us to conform to their standards
- pressures from people, situations, events, and circumstances over which we have no control

- worries about money and finances
- struggle to achieve and excel

No wonder our journey loses its savor and our sense of "God with us" disappears.

When God seems far away, who moved?

# 1

# That Nagging Feeling

So I am sure that God, who began this good work in you,
will carry it on until it is finished on the Day of Christ Jesus.
—Philippians 1:6, GNT

Have you ever hypnotized a chicken? It's easy. Hold a chicken on the ground, facedown, and put one hand on her back to keep her down. Then gently stretch out her neck so that her beak is flat against the ground. Still holding her in this position, make a line in the dirt extending from the end of her beak. Now let the chicken go.

She won't move. Why? Because she's hypnotized by that line in front of her. In fact, she'll lie there as if paralyzed until something finally breaks her focus—a loud noise, a sudden movement, or a breeze through her feathers.

That chicken is a good analogy for many Christians who are trying to cope with their lives and the world around them. A sense of purposelessness or lack of direction in their lives becomes the line in front of their nose that paralyzes them. Like the poor chickens my son, Nate, used to lay out around our barnyard, they are powerless.

This sense that things aren't going as they should comes to all of us. I once read a poem about the author's expectations for her future. She talked about a life of wealth and luxury, travel and privilege, and all the wonderful things she expected to happen in her life. I don't remember the author's name, but I do remember her final words:

> Yet, every so often I get this nagging feeling that I'm not headed in the Right Direction.

The nagging feeling that we're not headed in the right direction is a familiar one.

Sitting on the bus on the way to work one morning, I was overcome with a sense of futility and despair. I looked at my fellow commuters, each closed and shut off from the others. I thought of my office, the work that awaited me on my desk, the meeting I had with my boss. I thought of the angry words I had left behind as yet another argument with my teenager had erupted at the breakfast table. I remember thinking, *Who am I? How did I get here, in this place, with these people? Surely this isn't the powerful, victorious life that God has promised me?* I had that nagging feeling I wasn't headed in the right direction. As this feeling continued, I felt more and more out of touch with God, more and more alone on my personal faith journey.

Do you sometimes get a sense that where you are right now isn't where God intends you to be—that somewhere you took a wrong turn or headed in the wrong direction? Do you ever look around and ask yourself how you ended up where you are? Do you have moments when you wonder where God is?

## Stuck in a Rut

Perhaps you're feeling stuck in a rut of habit and complacency. All growth seems to have stopped in your job and in your relationships with family and friends. The trouble with a rut is that it's comfortable. It's easy. You don't have to think. But underneath stirs this nagging feeling.

When I moved from my city job to the country, I bought a small farm. The path to the woodlot skirted its way around two fields, over a rocky outcropping, and along the edge of the cedar bush. Two deep ruts marked the route, and if you set the wheels of a vehicle in them, it would practically drive itself up to the woodlot.

*In our Christian walk, it's only when we step off the broad and easy road that we discover the joys God has for us.*

Feeling adventurous one day, the kids and I decided to walk home along the fence line that disappeared into the cedar bush and reappeared in the field behind the barn. The cedar bush seemed impenetrable, but as we walked past the first two trees, we discovered a narrow, hidden pathway, overgrown and neglected. Pushing aside the branches that had grown over the path, we came to an open clearing. After the shadowy pathway, the sunlight in the clearing seemed doubly bright. We were confronted with a breathtaking sight. Towering cedars surrounded daisy-strewn grass, making a perfect oval. Protected by the tall sentinels, the clearing was hushed and still. Someone had made rustic benches, now moss-covered and weathered, along the edges. At one end, three tall cedars stood out from the perimeter, forming a natural altar.

After I met Gerald and we decided to get married, we had the ceremony in that "chapel" on my country property.

In our Christian walk, it's only when we step off the broad and easy road that we discover the joys God has for us. It takes courage to leave the comfortable rut (novelist Ellen Glasgow once said that the only difference between a rut and a grave is six feet) and step out boldly. However, this is when you feel that tingling sense of God with you as you begin to fulfill God's purpose for your life—rather than just spinning your wheels in the same old place.

# Out of Balance

Sometimes it isn't the rut that gives us that sense of heading in the wrong direction; it's the feeling that our lives are out of balance. Maybe you're overwhelmed by all the demands on your life: demands from your family, your friends, your job; demands from all the things you do day in and day out. You feel out of step with God.

My friend Janet had a poster in her kitchen that read "As soon as the rush is over, I'm going to have a nervous breakdown. I've worked hard for it. I deserve it, and nobody is going to deprive me of it." We used to laugh at it; but deep down, I recognized the desperation in the words. How can we walk with God when our lives are filled with so many things—schedules and appointments, clocks and Day-Timers—that keep us rushing and doing, coming and going? Most of us hit the ground running in the morning and don't stop until we fall into bed at night—exhausted.

*How can we walk with God when our lives are filled with so many things that keep us rushing and doing, coming and going?*

Did you know that bumblebees are workaholics? Not only does the young bumblebee begin working at an earlier age than a honeybee (forty-eight hours as opposed to two weeks), but he also puts in longer hours, often pulling an all-nighter if the night is clear. He literally works himself to death. The typical bumblebee wears himself out in four weeks.

Some of us are like bumblebees. We need to stop and smell the flowers now and then.

When I worked for a large computer corporation, we were constantly told, "It's a tough marketplace out there. You've got to fight to win." The world was seen as a giant battlefield on which wars are won and lost. The winners are rewarded with more pay, more responsibilities, more promotions, . . . and more battles. In this kind of world, spiritual matters often take a backseat.

# A Deeper Spiritual Life

Perhaps you're feeling the need for some spiritual growth. You may be successful in your career and happy in your relationships, but you still have a sense that there must be more to the Christian walk than what you've experienced. There's that nagging feeling again.

Somewhere along the way when I wasn't looking, I became rather sophisticated about my Christian experience. I'd like to think that it is a maturing of my faith, but I suspect that it's more like a hardening of the arteries that once flowed with living water. I can remember the wonder of those first days after I was roundly and soundly converted: the sky was bluer, the grass was greener, and I was excited about my newfound Lord. An older Christian smiled at my youthful enthusiasm when I told him what had happened to me. "Oh yes," he mused, "I used to be just like you, but now I've matured in my faith."

In retrospect, I'm sure there was a note of wistfulness in his voice, and now I know why. As an older Christian, I yearn for those heady days at the beginning of my walk with God. Somehow I got the idea that being a mature Christian means being a dull Christian. I'm glad to say that I've moved on. I'm learning to embrace opportunities to deepen my spiritual life—books, films, retreats, lectures, even an evangelist or two. Some of them are a little off the beaten path, but each one opens doors that lead me to a new walk with God.

If you're looking for a deeper spiritual life, then be prepared for a change in how you live that spiritual life. The comfortable roads will be gone, and before you will be a new, exciting—and scary—vista.

Sometimes in our lives, usually after a watershed event when everything is turned upside down, it seems as if the pathway before us is dark and unknown. Rather than step out, we hold back, hoping to hear a voice in the darkness as we wait for the light to shine.

When I moved to the country, I discovered what real darkness is. One night, I heard a strange noise from the barn and decided to investigate. The sky was overcast with clouds, but the light from the house windows lit up the path. I managed to grope my way to the barn, and I found a stray chicken who needed a little help to find her roost.

I closed the barn door and stood in the yard, marveling at the quietness of the night. Without warning, the house lights went out. I was in the dark, literally. And what a dark! Black, velvety, tangible dark around me. No light reflected from a shiny surface. No small beam or glow pierced the black wall surrounding me. I didn't dare move.

Several moments passed before I had the presence of mind to yell to someone in the house to turn the lights on. During those few moments I knew what it was to feel lost and helpless.

Sometimes on my Christian journey I have the same experience. Suddenly it feels as if all the lights have been turned off, and I am alone in the dark, left to stumble on as best I can. That's exactly how my life seemed after my divorce. I stumbled on in the dark, wondering where God had gone, trying to find my way through unknown territory. It wasn't until I stopped and yelled to God to turn the lights on that things changed.

Late one night I couldn't sleep. I was lonely, unhappy, and afraid, trying to make a life and a living for myself and two small children. I got up, wandered into the living room, and turned on the television. Inwardly I was praying, asking where God was and asking why I felt so alone and deserted. The television flared to life, and on the screen a small man in a white suit stood in the middle of a stage talking about his experience of God taking him up into the heavens. As he continued in his Southern twang, lights were skillfully manipulated so that the set darkened, stars came out, and his white suit glowed—in short, a hokey (to me) televangelist performance complete with organ and choir. Coming from a middle-of-the-road church background, I saw this as the antithesis of what I was used to. I was so angry at God! I'd asked for help, and God had given me . . . this!

Despite my anger, I began to listen to the man as he preached. And in his words was everything I needed to hear. God loved me. God will never desert me. God is with me. God will lead me. The light shone in my darkness.

Where you are right now in your faith walk may not seem to be what God has in mind for you or what you have in mind for yourself. But be assured, the first step in the practice of walking with God is to recognize that this moment, this place, this time, is a step on your path to heaven.

*You have to start somewhere, and where you are right now is that somewhere.*

You may be thinking that this can't possibly be true for you. Your life is a mess—your personal relationships are failing, your prayer life is nil, your sense of God's presence is gone. How can this be where God wants you to be?

This isn't where God *wants* you to be—it's where God can begin to work in you if you will allow it. You have to start somewhere, and where you are right now is that somewhere. It may take a gigantic leap of faith for you to believe this; but once you have come to the place where you can admit that your present circumstances are what God has to work with, then you can begin to walk closely with God.

One year I thought I finally had my garden under control. I mulched and double dug the beds, prepared them with loving care. The seeds, ordered months before and planted in little pots, were now sturdy seedlings ready for planting. The month was June and the weather was ideal. I weeded and fertilized and watered. On June 29, without warning, we had a hard frost. Most of the garden was wiped out. Undaunted, I replanted as much as I could.

On July 14 my newly sprouting garden was hit by a freak hailstorm. I walked away in despair.

Then, in late August, curiosity drove me to my garden. Underneath a tangle of weeds and tall grass, I found tomatoes, cucumbers, squash, corn, potatoes, turnips, carrots, and green peppers. They were not as big or as beautifully formed as I had planned, but they were there!

If you despair that your life seems like my garden—frostbitten and hail-battered—remember that the seed is still there and, in God's good time, will produce fruit.

Many people would rather wait until they get into a more suitable place to begin their daily faith walk with God. They'd rather clean up their relationships, begin to pray with discipline, wait until they sense God's presence before they try to move on. They're like dieters who want to start their new diet "when the time is right." Take it from me: it will never happen. Frankly speaking, if you're waiting until you feel "right," what will happen to your waiting if you're hit by a bus on the way home today? You will have missed the opportunity.

"Now is the time of God's favor, now is the day of salvation" (2 Cor. 6:2, NIV). It can't be any plainer than that!

Right now, in this place and time, who and what you are is the beginning of a closer walk with God.

## Group Exercise

Look at the following group of letters and read the words you see:

IAMNOWHERE

What words did the majority of the group read? How else can you read this cluster of letters?

The two places are the same; the difference is your perception. Either you are *nowhere*—at a dead end, unable to move or change your life, or you are *now here*—at a beginning point. All new journeys begin at a *now here* point, and so will yours—that is, if you will see your present position in that way.

## Questions for Group Discussion or Private Reflection

1. What plans did you have for your life when you were a child? How did you picture your future?
2. Where has your life made detours you might not have expected?
3. At what times in your life were you convinced that you weren't heading in the right direction? What red flags made you feel this way?
4. How are you feeling about the direction of your life today?
5. What is your faith walk with God like? Is it all you'd like it to be?

## Prayerful Concerns

Loving God, I trust that who I am today and where I am today are the perfect starting points for a closer walk with you. I thank you for the journey so far, and I praise you for the journey to come. Walk with me, I pray. Help me move ever closer to you as we journey together. Amen.

## For Your Journal

Keeping a journal is a great way to draw closer to God. If the idea of journaling is new to you, these guidelines will get you started:

- Use a specific book for your journal exercises.
- Keep it handy so you can make entries when ideas or thoughts come to you.
- Date your entries. That way, you can easily look back to see what you were thinking at a particular time.
- Keep your journal private so that you don't have to edit your thoughts for someone else's perusal. Give yourself the freedom to be completely honest.

For your first journal entry, write across the top of the page:

I Am Someone Who . . .

Now sit back and think about yourself. What do you do? What do you wear? What do you like? What do you not like? What do you eat? What do you think about? What do you dream about? What kinds of people do you like and dislike? What is your lifestyle? Keep writing until you fill at least one page. When you've finished, you'll have a personal picture of who you are— not where you live or what you do for a living or what you own— but of who you are and what is important to you. This is an important first step in understanding that the person you are right now is exactly the person God wants to lead into a deeper faith. This is where a closer walk with God begins.

☼

## Three Things to Do Before Reading the Next Chapter

1. Tomorrow, wear something to work (or any other place you may go) that you've never worn there before. Choose something that is part of your life. You might choose a favorite old sweater, your grandfather's watch, a school ring, or a different pair of shoes. If others notice and comment on your choice, tell them why you're wearing this item. It's a way of connecting with the people around you in a different mode and sharing a bit of yourself with them.

   When I wore a Western-style shirt to work one day, I found myself telling a coworker about the square dancing club I belonged to. A subtle shift took place in our relationship as she realized there was more to me than just business. When you try this activity, you'll find that you add a new dimension to other people's perception of who you are, and in the process, free your-self from the box of that perception.

2. Choose a new route to a usual destination. Open up your senses and become aware of all the differences you can see, hear, or smell. Compare the two routes. Which one is more comfortable? Which one is more interesting? Why would you choose one over the other?

3. In your journal reflect on the following questions: What was your predominant feeling when you wore a different outfit or took a different route from your usual ones? How did other people react to you?

# 2
# What Are You Supposed to Be Doing Anyway?

Run your best in the race of faith, and win eternal life for yourself; for it was to this life that God called you when you firmly professed your faith before many witnesses.
—1 Timothy 6:12, GNT

When I was growing up, my family once made a trip to Boston, a journey of nearly eight hundred miles. We didn't want to waste any of our precious vacation time on the road, so the object was to get to Boston as quickly as possible. We started in the early morning and drove all through the day and night. We drove and drove and drove. We ate in the car; we slept in the car. We stopped for nothing except gas. The scenery whizzed by at a steady sixty miles an hour. After awhile, it all looked the same: billboards, telephone poles, and the endless white line disappearing over the horizon.

My mother called this kind of traveling "hurtling through space." That was exactly what it felt like. We were hurtling through space to reach our goal: Boston. When we finally arrived, everyone was exhausted, cranky, and miserable. I have few memories of Boston other than being dragged in protest

27

through the basement of Filene's department store and watching some swans on the Boston Common. I was just too tired from the journey to take in the experience.

We all have goals. In business, some of us may aspire to be a supervisor or an executive. In our personal lives, we may dream of a big house in the suburbs. The goal is a fixed reality, and everything else becomes a means of getting to the goal as quickly as possible. We work toward that goal, sweat for that goal, and want that goal more than anything else. Yet when we finally reach the goal, we often look around the corner office or out the windows of the new house, and say to ourselves, *Is this it? Is this all there is? Is this what I've worked so hard to achieve?*

Along the way, we've missed the journey.

Many of us spend our lives hurtling through space, not stopping to see, not stopping to taste, not stopping to enjoy the pleasures along the way. We keep our eyes on the goal, aiming toward it with single-minded determination. And if we happen to run over a few people on the way or pass up a nice little side road or miss a parade or two, well, that's life, we say. It's short-term pain for long-term gain, we tell ourselves.

The goals we set are really the benefits of living, not the reason for living. Our reason for living is to know and worship God, not the goals we strive to attain. That's why so many people feel empty and cheated when they finally achieve those goals.

Moving toward God's purpose in your life is exactly the opposite of hurtling through space. The destination—heaven—is important but not the only reason for the journey. Getting there is more than half the fun; getting there is *all* the fun! The direction you take—what we call God's purpose—and the spirit in which you follow it make the difference between a goal-centered life and a purpose-centered life.

When you get that nagging feeling that you're not headed in the right direction, God's Spirit anxiously wants to speak to you and help you find the direction your life should take. You often miss clues right in front of your nose. Use these four guideposts to determine the right direction for your life:

1. The things you do well.
2. The times when you've sensed God's presence.
3. The times when doors opened for you—physically, mentally, or spiritually.
4. The things you yearn to do.

Let's start with what you do well.

## What Do You Do Well?

Most people tend to focus on their shortcomings and their weaknesses rather than on their talents and strengths. It's easy to make a list like this:

I'm not good at . . .
I can't do . . .
I could never . . .
I'm not . . .

Focusing on your weaknesses is like building your house on the sand. As in the biblical example, the wind and the rain will easily destroy whatever you build, and you'll be left wondering just what it is that God wants you to do.

For some of us, talking about personal strengths seems too much like bragging, so we tend to downplay them. What we're doing, though, is taking the credit away from God, who gave us these wonderful strengths, talents, and skills to use for the glory of God's name. We should be proud of the gifts God has given us and enjoy telling others of God's grace and bounty.

God gives you gifts and talents, which you can either use or ignore. These gifts and talents are specifically for you, and they are part of God's purpose for your life. If you have a lovely voice, you're probably already singing in a choir, bringing pleasure to others as you praise God. If you're good with children, you may be the neighborhood "guardian angel" or a Sunday school teacher.

Gifts and talents like these may be obvious. However, others are not so obvious. *Oh, I don't do anything well. I'm not very talented, I guess,* you may be thinking. Think again. God has given each one of us special gifts for glorifying God.

> Now there are varieties of gifts, but the same Spirit; and there are varieties of activities, but it is the same God who activates all of them in everyone.—1 Corinthians 12:4-6, NRSV

What do you do well? Do you bake the best chocolate chip cookies in the world? Do you listen to an elderly neighbor's long-winded stories? Do you keep everything organized at home or at the office? Do you always find something to laugh at, even amidst chaos? Do you remember everyone's anniversaries and birthdays?

When you look beyond the obvious gifts that most people think of—gifts like music, art, leading, teaching—to the gifts that reflect the person within, you'll find that God has endowed you with a multitude of wonderful talents. Preparing comforting food, listening when others won't, bringing order around you, giving laughter and humor, caring for people—these are great gifts that reflect the love of God through you.

The secret is to do these things with a strong sense of doing them for God. An old nun, Sister Jean, once told me, "Whatever you do in life, no matter how big or how small, offer it up to God." What a concept! Whether you're baking for your family or for the church bake sale, listening to your teenager or an old man on the bus, organizing a picnic or an office file system, regardless of whether it seems "important" or "spiritual" or "relevant," what would happen if you simply offered up every time you use your particular gift? Can you see how those things you do every day would become part of the larger direction of your life?

If you use your strengths—or gifts—as guideposts, you can begin to discern your life's direction in relation to these strengths.

For example, if you're a great organizer, then you can confidently expect a direction that requires organizational skills will allow you to fully express your gift.

Many will quote Paul, who says in his weakness he is made strong by God. Yes, this is true, but that truth usually manifests itself when we are "not heading in the right direction." Shortly after my divorce, with two small children to raise, I was desperate for work. Having been out of the business world for some time, I had little confidence that I was employable. I answered an ad for a teacher of English grammar and typing at the local business school. I was hired.

*If you use your strengths, or gifts, as guideposts, you can begin to discern your life's direction in relation to these strengths.*

Imagine my horror when I discovered that the administration also expected me to teach bookkeeping. *Me? The girl who failed fourth-grade math and never caught up after that?* But I needed the job, so I threw myself on God's mercy, and together we taught bookkeeping. Like Paul, I learned that in my weakness I was made strong by God. After that, I moved on to jobs more in line with my skills and talents.

## When Have You Sensed God's Presence?

How else can you be sure your direction in life is the right one? Think about the times when you were aware of God's presence with you—when you felt strong and powerful, empowered and confident. There may not be many examples that come to mind immediately. These are mountaintop experiences, and they serve as guideposts for your life direction.

Consider when you experienced such moments. Was it when you coped with an emergency, keeping your head when everyone else panicked? Perhaps your mountaintop moments weren't so dramatic. You may have felt this wonderful sense of empowerment while leading a Sunday school class, speaking to a group of people, or enjoying the satisfaction of a job well done.

One of my most memorable peak experiences occurred when I was asked to speak to a large group of Christian women. When it was time to travel to the meeting, my car wouldn't start, so I had to take our old truck into the city, a distance of sixty miles. Halfway there, I noticed I had very little gas. It was a Sunday, so I desperately drove around until I finally found an open gas station. I got gas and went on to the venue. Because the parking lot was crowded, I had to park several blocks from the building. By the time I arrived at the front door, I had only seconds to spare. I mounted the stage, stood behind the podium, and, in a moment of pure panic, realized I'd left my notes in the truck! I had no choice—I just "let go and let God." What a wonderful experience. The words seemed to roll off my tongue. The audience responded accordingly. They laughed when I was being funny; they cried when I tugged at their heartstrings. I knew that God was with me.

Similarly, your right direction probably will be in the areas where God is able to use you directly. Unlike this experience I had, a peak experience is not always at a time when God uses you directly. However, it's always at a time when you are aware of "God with you." It's as if what you are doing, however mundane or unspiritual, is transformed by a feeling of God's presence and care. The flat plain of life becomes a mountaintop.

## When Have Doors Opened for You?

Another guidepost for determining the right direction of your life is recognizing times when doors have opened for you—spiritually, mentally, and physically. I've always told people that if they're seeking a new direction in life, they should start knocking on doors.

I'm convinced that God is powerful enough to keep the door closed if a particular direction is not right for someone. When you knock on the door—that is, take the first few steps in the new direction—and that door opens wide, you know you're making the right move. If you have to sweat and strain, try and try again, go through hoops and trials, then perhaps God is trying to tell you something.

I've always been a good "door knocker." I'll write that letter, make that phone call, answer that ad, talk to that person—whatever it takes to move in the direction of whatever I believe God is asking me to do. If no one answers my letters; if no one is at the other end of the phone; if I get a negative reply to my inquiry; if a person won't talk to me, I consider the door closed and move on. It's a lot easier than just sitting and dreaming about what might be.

Interesting things can happen when that door I've knocked on suddenly opens. I may find myself in a situation where I truly have no hope except in the Lord. The door swings open, and I discover that I really wasn't committed to following through in the situation. I once left a secure job for a tenuous position involving a major upheaval, a change of workplace, and a whole new lifestyle. Why? Because the "door" to the new job was there, and I knocked. Much to my surprise (and secret horror), the door flew open and I was catapulted through into a whole new walk with God. When I look at where I am now, I can trace it directly to that particular open door. As David Lloyd George said, "Don't be afraid to take a big step if one is indicated. You can't cross a chasm in two small jumps."

> *I'm convinced that God is powerful enough to keep the door closed if a particular direction is not right for someone.*

# What Do You Yearn to Do?

Finally, when determining the right direction for your life, look at what you yearn to do. *Yearn* is the perfect word: a movement toward, a leaning, a wistful longing, a desire. I believe the Holy Spirit whispers within you and gives you yearnings for what is right for you. What do you yearn for? What situations? What people? What circumstances in life?

So often people tell me they've "always wanted to . . . ," but can't "because . . ." (excuses are myriad). If you've experienced a prolonged yearning for something, it's time to start moving in that direction. You won't learn to play the piano overnight, but you can sign up for a beginner's class at the local music school.

When it comes to finding the right direction for your life, taking the beaten track is always a lot easier than trailblazing. We had a ten-acre field for our five donkeys. At two acres per donkey, they had ample room for pasture and grazing. When I first turned them loose into the field, I expected each one to stake out its own territory. Give five humans ten acres, and they'll immediately start to build fences. But not the donkeys. They created pathways like spider webs across the field, each exactly one-donkey wide. The paths became smooth and easy to navigate. The rocks were kicked aside, the paths were smoothed down, and the obstacles circumnavigated. Sadly, over the years the field changed, and now the old trails bypass the fertile pasture areas.

Your life may be the same. It's so much easier to stick with what you know and follow the established way you've always done it; but if God's direction for your life lies outside your beaten track, you may have to consider a change of direction.

You may have already figured out that God isn't going to physically, bodily move you into the right direction. You must get moving and take the first steps yourself. However, knowing that you are following your own personal guideposts will make those steps off the beaten path less frightening. Then you can be assured of moving in a way that allows God to guide you as you travel farther on the journey.

## Group Exercise

- Briefly share reflections on the previous chapter's "Things to Do" exercises.
- Imagine your house is on fire. All people and animals have been rescued. The fire fighter announces you have time to save three things but no more. Size and weight are not important. What three things would you rescue? Why? Ask group members what these things may say about who you are.

## Questions for Group Discussion or Private Reflection

1. In your previous journal exercise ("I am a person who . . ."), you may have discovered strengths you never recognized before. What are your personal strengths (gifts)?
2. When have you been aware of God's presence with you? What were you doing? How did you feel?
3. When did you "knock on the door" and take the first step in a new direction? What happened? How do you feel about that today?
4. What do you yearn for? (Note: Don't be shy about opening up and telling others some of your private yearnings. You may find they will have suggestions about how to move in that direction.)
5. In what ways are you still sticking to the beaten track in your life? Why?

## Prayerful Concerns

Gracious God, thank you for the gifts you have given me. I may not have acknowledged them before, but I do so now, realizing I have received them through your loving bounty. Help me to use them wisely. Show me the path that I should take. Amen.

## For Your Journal

Make four columns on the page and write these headings: Gifts, Mountaintops, Doors, Yearnings. Reflect on each category and make notes on whatever comes to mind. You may find yourself writing about specifics or general comments. If you're feeling uncomfortable or negative about any category, note that. If you have an insight about yourself in relation to an area, write that down also. Take time to reflect fully on these guideposts.

When you finish, turn to a new page and write "Maybe God wants me to. . . ." Write everything that comes to mind. Don't analyze or refute anything. Write without judgment.

☼

## *Three Things to Do Before Reading the Next Chapter*

1. Intentionally use one of your strengths (gifts). That is, plan to exercise your gift, and as you do, thank God for it and the opportunity to express God's love for you through your gift.

2. Think of something you yearn for. Consider what door would help you move toward this desire or goal. Knock on that door: write, call, talk, answer, or inquire. See what happens.

3. Reflect in your journal on these questions: What happened when you exercised your gifts? Did you open a door for a yearning? What did you find out?

# 3
# Check Your Baggage

Let us rid ourselves of everything that gets in the way,
and of the sin which holds on to us so tightly, and let us
run with determination the race that lies before us.
— Hebrews 12:1, GNT

Two Buddhist monks were walking beside a stream that
had overflowed its banks. They saw a young woman
standing on the edge, obviously unable to cross the
swollen stream without getting her clothes wet. Without saying
anything, one monk simply scooped her up in his arms, walked
across the stream, and deposited her on the other side. The
monks continued on their way. At the end of the day when their
vow of silence could be broken, the second monk turned to the
first and said, "How could you touch that woman, knowing what
our vows are?" The first monk replied, "I put her down on the
other side of the stream, but you have been carrying her all day."

That is true for many of us. We carry things with us all day—
baggage that slows us down and prevents us from enjoying God's
presence in our lives.

# The Power of Core Convictions

If you look at the baggage cart of your life, you'll discover the biggest trunk holds your convictions. Convictions can be positive or negative, but it is your negative convictions that weigh a ton.

Where do these convictions come from? Early in your life, people communicated messages about your worth, your competency, your appearance, and your role in life. In short, they told you who you were. If you heard good and powerful messages, you developed a positive view of yourself. However, you probably didn't receive consistently positive messages. You may have heard that you were bright or friendly but also that you didn't measure up to the example set by an older sister; that you were too slow, too emotional, or too silly. The messages from significant people in your life established the starting points for your internal convictions and act as predictors of your behavior today. They were the seeds of your conviction structure.

*The messages you received from significant people in your life established the starting points for your internal convictions and act as predictors of your behavior today.*

When I was a child, my mother, a tiny woman, continually told me I was going to grow up to look like one of my aunts—an enormously overweight woman. From my mother's point of view, I did look large since I'd inherited my father's big bones and stocky build. However, by the time I entered my teens, I had a core conviction that I was doomed to obesity. For decades I struggled with my weight until one day when my pastor prayed for me; through the Holy Spirit I was set free from this negative conviction.

Today my weight no longer dominates my thoughts as it once did. I'll never be a tiny woman like my mother, but there's no reason to believe I'll be obese either.

Why are these negative messages so powerful in our lives? As a child, you had no filters for sorting out what was true and what wasn't true. You believed every message you heard equally. Your subconscious mind took these messages and made them true.

All these messages taken together form your core convictions. You never stop to think about a core conviction. You simply act on your mental programming. You can recognize a core conviction when you hear yourself say, "I always. . . ." For example, "I always fail at everything related to numbers."

Of course, some core convictions exert positive influences in your life, such as convictions about God's love, the sanctity of marriage, or the love of parent for child.

Three basic core convictions affect your life profoundly, depending on whether they are positive or negative:

1. Your core conviction about responsibility
2. Your core conviction about self-worth
3. Your core conviction about expectations

## Responsibility

What is your core conviction about responsibility? When situations don't work out the way you wish, do you blame other people? circumstances? situations? God? Do you decide whose fault it is? Is it the system's fault? Or the world's? Do you blame and label other people for what goes wrong in your life?

Are you like the four characters in *The Wizard of Oz?* They all had a core conviction that someone else was responsible for their unhappiness. The Cowardly Lion couldn't be brave; the Tin Man couldn't be caring; the Scarecrow couldn't be smart; and Dorothy couldn't find her way home. Why? Because someone hadn't given them courage, heart, brains, or empowerment. They were looking for someone to take responsibility for their lives. They were looking for the Wizard of Oz.

## Self-worth

You have a core conviction about self-worth, also called self-esteem. Do you feel lovable? Do you feel you deserve good things in your life?

I wasn't aware of this conviction in my own life until one day I realized that every time I had a negative experience, a little inner voice said, *Serves me right.* If I locked myself out of my car: *Serves me right.* If I spilled something on my suit two minutes before a big presentation, *Serves me right.* If I slammed my finger in the door, *Serves me right.* That voice repeated a strong message about what I felt I deserved in life.

What are you saying to yourself about your self-worth? Do you put yourself down? call yourself stupid? label yourself unworthy? Do you constantly remind yourself that you're worthless, useless, hopeless, and helpless? Or do you label yourself with comments such as, *I'm too . . . (too young, too old, too poor, too dumb)*?

*What are you saying to yourself about your self-worth?*

The impostor complex exemplifies a negative core conviction about self-worth carried to the extreme. A person works hard to achieve a goal of status or prestige. When he or she finally achieves the goal, the person feels unworthy. Even sitting in the president's chair in the president's office with the president's business cards and the president's salary, the person feels like an impostor deep inside because he or she believes, *I'm not worthy of this position.* It's like being Cinderella, waiting for the clock to strike twelve, knowing that the coach will turn into a pumpkin, the coachmen into mice, and you will be revealed as an impostor.

## Expectations

Your core conviction about expectations affects your view of the world. You've heard the old saying that people see the glass as either half empty or half full. One is a positive expectation; the other is negative. It's all in the way you look at life.

Someone told me her five key words are, "There is no free lunch." What a sad, pinched view of the universe this is. Do you believe you are part of a supportive, benevolent universe, a universe that gives you many free blessings every day: a smile from a stranger, love from friends, beautiful sunsets, starlit nights, and glimpses of glory all around?

Our expectations for life can be negative or positive. Do you expect to do well, to succeed, to live fully, to enjoy God's universe? I have a large poster in my office that reads, "Blessed are they who expect nothing, for they shall never be disappointed." How often do we hold back from a high expectation for something because we fear we will be disappointed? "How was the seminar?" "Just what I expected—dull and dry." No disappointment there, or is the disappointment in the expectation? Expect a lot, and a lot will come to you. Expect to have fun, and you will. Expect to enjoy a program, and it will be enjoyable.

*Expect a lot, and a lot will come to you. Expect to have fun, and you will.*

What are your expectations about people? Do you believe people are basically good and can be trusted? How do you relate to your fellow human beings? Many of the messages you received about people as a child carried over into adulthood. Helping children build positive expectations about people has become more difficult because today a loving, trusting child can be in danger. How do we tell our children "never speak to strangers" and at the same time tell them people are basically good? How do we tell the Bible story of the good Samaritan in a world where a "good Samaritan" can be sued by the stranger?

## Changing Negative Core Convictions

Negative core convictions can cause more harm than just being heavy baggage. They can hold us back from our true potential in Christ. They can destroy our sense that we are God's children and take away the joy of living the Christian life.

*Negative core convictions can cause more harm than just being heavy baggage. They can hold us back from our true potential in Christ.*

"As [a man] thinketh in his heart, so is he" (Prov. 23:7, KJV). That describes the effect of core convictions. What you think about on the inside is what you become on the outside. You become a self-fulfilling prophecy.

Three simple, practical steps can change a core conviction. The first step is to recognize the conviction. As you've been reading about core convictions, perhaps you have had an "aha!" moment when you thought, *So that's what's been going on. I didn't realize that was a conviction that I was dragging around as baggage.* Have you heard your inner spirit confirming your core conviction?

The second step is to question the conviction. Where did this conviction come from? Think about what you were told in the past that contributed to this negative core conviction. Where did your mental programming begin? What was said that gave you this negative conviction about yourself or your life?

Third, put a price on your conviction. What is this conviction costing you in your relationships, in your career, in your personal life, in your health, in your mental state, and in your walk with the Lord? As you begin to recognize the cost of negative convictions, you begin to see how they are affecting every area of your life.

If your core convictions came from the messages you heard in the past, you can change those convictions by changing the messages today. Your subconscious mind is still listening and continues to believe what it hears, just as it did when you were a child. Today you can speak to yourself with the words of Jesus, the most powerful words in the world.

Here are three powerful scriptures you can use. Write them on a card and put the card where you will continually see it. Repeat the scriptures to yourself often. Just as you continually heard the negative statements in the past, now you can continually give yourself the positive messages of your Savior.

To give yourself a new conviction about responsibility: "When he, the Spirit of truth, comes, he will guide you into all truth. He will not speak on his own; he will speak only what he hears, and he will tell you what is yet to come. He will bring glory to me by taking from what is mine and making it known to you" (John 16:13-14, NIV).

To give yourself a new conviction about your self-worth: "You are my friends if you do what I command. I no longer call you servants, because a servant does not know his master's business. Instead, I have called you friends, for everything that I learned from my Father I have made known to you. You did not choose me, but I chose you and appointed you to go and bear fruit—fruit that will last" (John 15:14-16, NIV).

To give yourself a new conviction about expectations: "So I say to you: Ask and it will be given to you; seek and you will find; knock and the door will be opened to you. For everyone who asks receives; he who seeks finds; and to him who knocks, the door will be opened" (Luke 11:9-10, NIV).

**Group Exercise**
- Briefly share reflections on the previous chapter's "Things to Do" exercises.
- Go around the group and complete the following phrases. Be sure to say what first comes to mind without weighing

whether the answer is right or wrong, good or bad, Christian or unchristian.

I'd be further ahead today if it weren't for . . .

When good things happen to me, I always . . .

When someone does something nice for me, I . . .

When looking forward to something, I tend to . . .

## Questions for Group Discussion or Private Reflection

1. When have you found yourself blaming other people, circumstances, or even God for your situation?
2. Do you think some people deserve good things more than others do? Why?
3. What do you expect from other people?
4. Do you view the world as a good place or a bad place? Why?

## Prayerful Concerns

Lord Jesus, I know I am bound and fettered by beliefs that do not reflect your love and care. I trust you to free me from these beliefs and, in their place, fill me with a conviction of my worth and lovableness. Amen.

## For Your Journal

Make three columns on the page and label them: People, Core Conviction, and Result.

In the first column write names of the influential people during the first ten years of your life: parents, siblings, relatives, neighbors, teachers, and so forth.

In the second column write the core convictions you received from these people. Put a plus sign next to those convictions you consider to be positive core and a minus sign next to those you consider to be negative.

In the last column note the results of these core convictions in your life today. How have they influenced how you feel, how you behave, and how you live your Christian life?

Across the bottom of the page write in block letters:

I AM GOD'S LOVED CHILD.

☼

## Three Things to Do
## Before Reading the Next Chapter

1. Some of us still have trouble dealing with the issue of self-worth. We find it hard to believe that, as one commercial puts it, we're "worth it"! I remember walking down the supermarket aisle with a good friend. We came to the bakery where pecan tarts were on sale. "Oh, I love pecan tarts," she said, "but I never buy them because no one else in the house likes them." Choose to give yourself a little treat—something special just for you. Tell yourself, "I am God's loved child, and I deserve it."

2. Become aware of expectations. Listen to others and hear how often they express negative expectations for a coming event or situation. Make a point to reverse the expectations, putting them in a positive light.

3. Reflect in your journal on the following questions: What treat did you give yourself? What was your initial feeling about this exercise? How do you feel about it now? Were you able to change negative expectations to positive ones? What happened? How did other people react?

# 4

# Who's Shoulding on You?

Do you, my friend, pass judgment on others? You have
no excuse at all, whoever you are. For when you judge
others and then do the same things which they do, you
condemn yourself.

—Romans 2:1, GNT

Have you ever been "should upon"? You know what I mean.
Either you or someone around you tells you what you should
do.

"Shoulding" starts early in life as the adults around us—our
parents, older siblings, relatives, schoolteachers, pastors, neighbors, the person in the grocery store, the crossing guard, the bus
driver—tell us what we should do in order to be okay.

"Children should be seen and not heard."

"Big boys shouldn't cry."

"You should share your toys with others."

"You should be more grateful."

"You should always wear clean underwear in case you're in an
accident."

"You should work harder in school."

"You should hurry up."

Over the years we take on a "should" for every situation in our lives. Soon the "should's" form a belief system that becomes an integral part of who we are and how we live in the world. Unfortunately, "should's" don't reflect the freedom we are offered as part and parcel of our Christian life. The "should's" bind us and take away the freedom of God's love. Before long we find ourselves full of despair and unhappy, wondering why life has no joy and everything seems such a grind. It's hard to walk close to God when you're being "should upon"!

No doubt you can reel off many "should's" you have heard from others and have incorporated into your life. However, four "should's" have the potential to tie a Christian up in knots. I tell people these "should's" are the Enemy's favorite weapons.

## "You Should Be Perfect"

Maybe it happened when you came running in from school with your math test and excitedly told your mother that you got 99 out of 100 answers correct. If your mother replied, "What happened to the other one?" the Be-Perfect "should" was born.

I once went to a dinner party hosted by a friend who obviously was driven by the Be-Perfect "should." The tableware was perfect, the settings were perfect, the guest list was perfect, the food was perfect. Just as we sat down to eat, he suddenly turned white. He stood up and shouted at his wife, "You forgot the napkins, and I wanted this dinner to be perfect." He spoiled the dinner not only for himself but for his guests and his wife. A napkin kept him from enjoying the evening.

I didn't realize I had allowed the Be-Perfect "should" to infiltrate my life. In fact, I always prided myself on the fact that I was anything but a perfectionist. However, when I faced an emergency surgery for possible cancer, the real truth emerged. I had only two days before the scheduled surgery. Did I spend them enjoying my family, doing things I loved to do? Did I spend them in prayer and meditation? No. I spent them cleaning my house.

Why? Well, I couldn't bear the thought that I might not make it, and then people would see the real Pat—the one with the messy linen closet and the unpolished silver, not the perfect Pat I wanted them to think I was. So I cleaned the toilets, ironed my linens, and polished the silver. Somehow, somewhere, I had gotten the idea that I should be a perfect housekeeper in order to be an okay person. How sad!

Read these statements and mentally check any you agree with.

I never start anything if I think I might fail at it.

I'd rather do it myself than let someone else do a poor job.

I constantly push myself to higher and higher levels of perfectionism.

I tend to grade myself, and I usually fall short of 100 percent.

I hate to fail at anything.

I often feel like collapsing under my internal pressure to succeed.

I can't stand the feeling that I don't quite measure up to others' expectations of me.

I can feel all right only when everything is neat, orderly, tidy, and perfect.

I need to keep my life under control with lists, schedules, and timetables that must be followed.

Perfection is worth striving for in this life. I encourage my family to strive for it, too.

It's important to set high standards and not settle for less.

If you felt comfortable with these statements and agreed with many, you may have a Be-Perfect "should" telling you how to run your life.

Here's the rub: nothing in life will be perfect. Perfection isn't attainable, because it is determined by the point of view of others.

I've always prided myself on my seafood chowder. In fact, I think it's just about perfect. I served it to two friends for lunch. One said it was "perfect," except it needed a little more salt. The other declared it "perfect," except she found it a little salty. Two bowls of chowder: two standards of perfection. I could never make a chowder that would please both people perfectly.

*Perfection isn't attainable, because it is determined by the point of view of others.*

People who are compelled by a Be-Perfect "should" cannot understand that their pursuit of perfection is doomed from the outset, and as a result, they live frustrated and unhappy lives. In their Christian witness, they become holier-than-thou, judgmental Pharisees, eager to "should upon" people around them in order to make themselves look perfect.

## "You Should Be Strong"

Another "should" can prevent us from enjoying our daily walk with God. Some of us allow the Be-Strong "should" to rule our lives. The Be-Strong "should" takes control when we are told that to be open and vulnerable is to be in danger. Perhaps you had an experience as a child where you learned that the only way to protect yourself was to be tough, strong and independent. Perhaps you heard: "You should act like a man"; "You should grow up"; "You shouldn't be such a crybaby."

The Be-Strong "should" doesn't necessarily mean you are tough or demonstrate intestinal fortitude. Instead, it means you keep a tight lid on your emotions and close yourself off from others. This "should" tells you not to show how you feel, to avoid getting too close to others, and to keep your feelings to yourself.

I've observed people governed by the Be-Strong "should" in church groups. You probably have as well. They are the ones who sit down when everyone is standing up, fold their arms when others are lifting theirs, and snort disdainfully when others are crying.

The Be-Strong "should" creates people who are tough on the outside but dying of loneliness on the inside. They long for the touch of another human being, but they don't allow anyone to get close enough to touch them for fear of being hurt, dismissed, despised, used, or abused.

They often become those Christians who seem to have missed the joy in their Christian walk. Buttoned-down, uptight, serious, they criticize "emotional" people who hug each other, laugh when they're happy, cry when they're sad, and obviously enjoy their walk with the Lord.

Read these statements and mentally check any you agree with:

I hate showing my true emotions. I'd rather keep them to myself.

I find it almost impossible to open up to people, including those close to me.

I think I should be able to handle my problems by myself. I hate to ask for help, especially on the personal level.

I get embarrassed when I'm around other people who are expressing strong emotions.

I get uncomfortable if someone gets too close to me on a personal level.

Other people complain that it is hard to get to know me.

I often feel nothing in highly emotional situations.

Sometimes I act as if I'm angry when something affects me deeply.

It's important for me to keep my emotions under control.

If you felt comfortable with these statements and agreed with many, you may have a Be-Strong "should" telling you how to run your life.

## "You Should Work Hard"

My son, Nathan, decided that he was going to enter the school's science fair. For weeks, he talked about the fair and how great it was going to be. However, I never saw him actually working on his project. The night before the entries were due, he disappeared into his bedroom. The next morning, Nathan left for school with his project in a pillowcase.

That evening he rushed into the house full of pride. "Guess what, Mom," he said. "I won first prize in my category."

"That's great," I replied, and then before I could stop myself, I "should upon" him. "But do you think you put in enough effort for first prize? You should work hard on a project." For some reason it seemed wrong to me that he won with so little effort. What about those kids who had put in hours and hours on their projects? Didn't they deserve more because of their efforts?

The Work-Hard "should" communicates that nothing in life comes without a great deal of effort. It says, "Life is a grind and then you die." It tells you that if it tastes good, it's not good for you; that only hard work earns a reward. Sometimes this "should" comes disguised as a work ethic; many workaholics are simply people driven by a Work Hard "should."

Christians driven by the Work-Hard "should" work hard at being Christians. They obey all the rules—and miss all the fun. The story of Mary and Martha is a classic example of a Work Hard person "shoulding" all over someone who doesn't have the same belief. Martha got angry when she noticed Mary enjoying herself with the guests while she did all the work herself. She felt compelled to "should" all over Mary.

The same thing happens in numerous church kitchens. The Marthas are busy in the kitchen (usually the same persons each time) while the Marys are swanning around outside, enjoying themselves. Before you know it, being a good worker becomes synonymous with being a good Christian.

Read these statements. Do any of them resonate with you?

I think results reflect how much work was put into the project.

Nothing of real value comes easily in this life.

I don't feel that I'm where I should be in life, considering how hard I've worked.

I sometimes feel like a victim, struggling against overwhelming odds.

Life is a struggle.

I feel pushed to work harder and harder.

I think other people have no idea how hard I work.

Work is not supposed to be fun; it's work!

It's important to work hard at everything.

If you felt comfortable with these statements and agreed with many, you may be a victim of the Work Hard "should."

## "You Should Please Others"

The Please-Others "should" is the most insidious driver of all. That's because it sounds so Christian! It's doing unto others as you would have them do to you and loving your neighbor all rolled up in one—except there is no love, no desire, and no pleasure involved!

People who hear the Please-Others "should" in their lives are usually frustrated by their inability to say no. They find themselves trapped in various situations, doing things they really don't want to do, simply to please others. They canvass for charities, bake cookies for the youth group, answer the telephones at the help center, help out in the nursery, serve at the coffee hour, and hand out welcome baskets. There's nothing wrong with any of these activities—if they're done with joy and pleasure and a real sense of service. But if people do these jobs because they feel they "should" do them, the personal value is gone.

People pleasers can't do anything just for themselves. If they buy something for themselves (and that's a long process involving a lot of guilt and second-guessing), they also buy gifts for everyone else to justify their "selfish" purchase.

People pleasers feel responsible for the happiness of everyone around them. They plan family activities with an anxious heart, hoping that everything will please everyone (an impossible task to begin with), and if anything goes wrong, they're quick to take the blame and say, "I'm sorry." They draw little pleasure themselves from these activities since they spend every moment watching to see how everyone else is doing.

Read these statements and mentally check any you agree with:

I think people often take advantage of me.

I feel responsible for those around me.

I get depressed if I think someone doesn't like me or is angry with me.

I feel bad if others are not satisfied with my efforts to please them.

I can't seem to say no to other people's demands.

I want people to like me, and I'll work hard toward that goal.

I feel guilty if I do something just for me and don't do something for those around me as well.

I know exactly how other people are feeling, but no one ever seems to know how I feel.

I tend to take on other people's worries and problems.

I often push aside my own needs and feelings in order to cope with other people's feelings and needs.

It's important to please others and make them happy.

The "should's" in our lives demand the impossible from us. They buoy us up by false motivation—a pressure that has no connection to our inner spirit. They ultimately sap our energy, halt our momentum, and separate us from God. Unfortunately these same "should's" also seem virtuous on the surface: perfection, strength, hard work, and selflessness. By their very nature, "should's" seem to be right. But, by their very nature, "should's" are false: they are based on an assumption that we won't be able to live up to the standard, so guilt is inevitable. Here's how a "should" really works:

"I should spend more time with my family." I don't have more time, so I don't spend more time, and so I feel guilty because "I should spend more time with my family."

"I should lose some weight." I fall off a diet again, so I don't lose the weight, and so I feel guilty because "I should lose some weight."

"I should read the Bible every day." I read the Bible for three days, miss a day, read one day, miss four days, and I feel guilty because "I should read the Bible every day."

## Group Exercise

- Briefly share reflections on the previous chapter's "Things to Do" exercises.
- Play the "should upon" game. Starting with the leader of the group, turn to the person on your left and say, "You should . . ." Complete the statement with a well-known maxim, such as, "You should eat your vegetables." Continue around the group and see how long you can keep the game going. Inject a few Christian "should's" as well, such as, "You should read the Bible every day."

### Questions for Group Discussion or Private Reflection
1. What is one "should" you can still hear one of the adults in your early life saying to you?
2. How has that "should" affected your life today?
3. How do you "should upon" others? How do they react?
4. Do you operate under any of the "should's" discussed in this chapter? How have they affected your walk with the Lord? How do they make you feel?

### Prayerful Concerns
Merciful God, I do not need to be "should upon" by anyone, for you alone determine who or what I am and where and how I live. Give me the power to accept that freedom. I ask this in Jesus' name. Amen.

### For Your Journal
Begin a two-part exercise dealing with the "should's" in your life. Follow directions here for the first part; the second part is described in the next chapter.

Divide the page into four columns, and label them Should, Action, Permission, Freedom.

Before beginning to write, sit quietly and think back to your childhood. Hear the voices of your parents, your older siblings, your teachers, your friends, and adults in your life. In the first column write the "should's" you hear.

In the second column write any ways in which these "should's" have affected your life today, particularly in how you act or react to the people, places, events, and situations in your life.

On a fresh page write your reactions to doing this part of the exercise. What are your emotions, your thoughts, your revelations, your "aha's"?

In the second part of the exercise, found in the next chapter, you will come back to the page with fresh insights on how to free yourself from the "should's" in your life and begin to walk in the fullness and freedom of God's love.

# Three Things to Do
# Before Reading the Next Chapter

1. Count the "should's." Keep a tally sheet nearby and count every time you hear the word *should*, either from yourself or from others. You can do this for one day, or—if you'd like a challenge—try doing it for several days. You'll be amazed (or appalled) by how often the word is used.

2. Say no to a request. It doesn't matter what you choose to say no to. Take note of how you feel when you say no.

3. Reflect in your journal on the following questions: What did you discover when you counted "should's"? Did you find you were equally guilty of "shoulding" on others? Who is the greatest "shoulder" in your life? Did you say no? What happened? How do you feel about the exercise?

# 5
# The Sound of a Distant Drum

For we conclude that a person is put right with God only
through faith, and not by doing what the Law commands.
—Romans 3:28, GNT

Do you ever feel as if everyone is telling you how you should
live your life? Family members have their expectations of
you—what you should do, what you should be. Society
has expectations—how you should behave, how you should fit in.
At your workplace, "should's" govern every situation (called Standard Operating Procedures by some); at church, the "should's"
surround you.

As we noticed in the previous chapter, some of the "should's"
*seem* fine: You should work hard. You should be strong. You
should be perfect. You should please others. How can you argue
with statements that sound so right? So . . . you try to live up to
that "should." It's okay for the first few days. Then something
intervenes, and you slack off from your efforts, give in to your
emotions, make a mistake, or act selfishly. You didn't live up to the
"should." What is the result? Guilt!

That's the crux of the matter. A "should" brings guilt with it.

"I/you should stop eating so much junk food." I don't, and I
feel guilty as I stuff an supersize hamburger into my mouth.

"I/you should stop yelling at the kids." I don't, and I feel guilty even as I'm yelling at Number One Son to clean up his room.

"I/You should go back to school and upgrade your education." I don't, and I feel guilty as another year slips by.

Fear sets in. *I'll never measure up*, we say to ourselves. There goes the triumphant, victorious Christian life.

But guilt and fear are not what God planned for us. God sent Jesus to free us from the guilt and the resulting fear that paralyze so many Christians. Paul said it best, "For you did not receive a spirit of slavery to fall back into fear, but you have received a spirit of adoption" (Rom. 8:15, NRSV).

*God sent Jesus to free us from the guilt and the resulting fear that paralyze so many Christians.*

How can we become like those Christians who seem free of all worry and fear about what others think of them? They sing their own songs, dance their own dances, and go their own way. To paraphrase Thoreau, they march to the sound of a different drummer.

Rather than march to the drumbeats that sound so loudly around us—the drumbeat of society's expectations; the drumbeat of what our families want; the drumbeat of our own need to measure up and do well—perhaps we should be listening for the sound of the distant drum, the still small voice of God, speaking to us through the tumult and stress of our daily lives.

In that voice we will hear what I call divine permission giving us the freedom to sing our own song and dance our own dance. This divine permission tells us we are loved children of God and that no one is allowed to "should upon" us again.

## Permission to Make Mistakes

It's okay to fail. A 99 out of 100 is great! A clean house doesn't always signify a good homemaker. Mistakes happen. No one is perfect. Other people don't need to be corrected when they are wrong. It's all right to just let it go once in awhile.

Are you cringing as you read these statements? Perhaps in the last chapter, you became aware of a Be-Perfect "should" hanging over your shoulder. You may be a person who straightens up the magazines in the doctor's office, carries a red pencil to correct your employees' work, and cannot walk out of the house unless everything is tidy.

If that last paragraph describes you, probably you also want to be a perfect Christian. You feel free to correct others whose theology might be a little sloppy, always have a Bible verse or platitude ready if someone needs help, and make sure everyone knows how "religious" you are. You know what it takes to be a perfect Christian, and unfortunately most of the people in your church don't have it!

*It's not the magnitude of the sin that counts but the distance between us and God when we sin.*

Guess what? Neither do you. We're told in Romans 3:23 that everyone is a sinner. No amount of perfection-seeking behavior can overcome this basic fact. You're just as much a sinner as the murderer on death row, for according to the same verse, everyone falls short of God's glory. It's not the magnitude of the sin that counts but the distance between us and God when we sin.

Jesus also says he came to call sinners. Wow! Sinners! Not perfect people. Sinners—like you and me. You don't have to be perfect before you're called. You're called where you are right now.

Here is the divine permission that allows you to let go of an unyielding quest for an unattainable perfection: "But he said to me, 'My grace is sufficient for you, for my power is made perfect in weakness.' Therefore I will boast all the more gladly about my weaknesses, so that Christ's power may rest on me" (2 Cor. 12:9, NIV).

It is when we make mistakes that God's power is best seen in us. God is the perfecter, not us. What a burden to be lifted off our shoulders! We don't have to be perfect to be okay as Christians. We can make mistakes. We can screw up now and then. We can even fail, because we can always count on Jesus to redeem those mistakes and bring good from them.

## Permission to Be Weak

Not long ago I went to a movie that had a lot of emotional content. You know the kind, a chick flick. There was death and dying, romance and reunion, anger and love—an emotional gamut that wrung me out just watching. When I left the theater, I noticed a number of people surreptitiously wiping their eyes. However, one fellow behind me seemed to be angry. He commented loudly to his companion, "What a dumb movie! Never saw so much ridiculous carrying on in my life! All the characters weeping and wailing at every opportunity. They needed to get over it and get on with their lives! If we acted like that in real life, where would this world be?" I could tell he had his emotions under control. The Be-Strong "should" kept him in line.

I have a confession to make. I used to be that kind of person. Early in life I learned to keep my emotions buttoned down. Being an only child and coming from a broken home (as it was called then), I was drilled by my mother not to trust anyone else, to be tough and strong—able to take care of ourselves, not to let others know how we felt, and never to open ourselves to other people because that would only lead to more hurt. Of course, as an adult, I now recognize her attitude as the reaction to being deserted by my father. But at the time I learned the lessons well.

For years I kept myself to myself—tightly bottled up and afraid to show emotions or become emotionally involved with people. Only through the loving-kindness of two wonderful Christians, Ron and June Armstrong, did I learn it was okay to express emotions and connect with others. The divine permission is so simple: be like Jesus. What do we see in Jesus' behavior? We see that Jesus expressed his feelings:

He probably laughed at wedding celebrations he enjoyed with his companions.

He wept when he looked down over Jerusalem.

He got angry at the money changers in the temple.

He felt pity for the afflicted people around him.

He loved deeply when he raised Lazarus from the dead.

He felt fear as he prayed in Gethsemane.

How do we know all this? Because Jesus allowed others to see his emotions. He didn't bottle himself up; rather, he poured himself out—so much so that he often felt depleted and empty, needing rest and recovery. He was a man totally involved in what was going on at the moment. He left himself open and vulnerable to others and expressed his emotions freely. Jesus gave of himself even more freely. He was the ideal model of what it is to be open to others.

As Christians we are called to joyfully emulate this kind of living. Rather than stifle our emotions and feelings, we can express them as part of our Christian witness. If others ridicule us or laugh at us, if they try to hurt us or use us, it's not our problem but their problem. We can trust our Lord to take care of us.

## Permission to Enjoy Life

If you're living under the Work Hard "should," you know that life is hard. There are so many things that should be done, so many rules that should be obeyed, and so many obligations that should be met. The days are never long enough for you to get your "work" done.

In the context of church work, you often find yourself saying, "Well, somebody has to do it." And that somebody is frequently you. You're the one who ends up doing the work—missing the sermon as you make coffee for social hour; missing the social hour fellowship as you clean up the kitchen; missing the sunshine on the church steps as you sweep out the hall.

Is that how it goes with you? Church isn't fun—it's work. You're annoyed that so many people are willing to let you do all the work. It just isn't fair! No doubt, you take the opportunity to let other people know they "should" be working in the church, not just enjoying it. "If I have to work here in the kitchen, you should feel guilty because you're not here with me." That's the kind of message communicated by many people driven by the Work Hard "should."

*Somewhere deep inside you may be feeling your works will earn you heavenly rewards.*

Why are you working hard? Is it because you believe you'll earn the red-carpet treatment when you reach the pearly gates? You'll be first in line, way ahead of all those sluggards who lounged around and didn't do anything to earn their golden crowns. You may think I'm going overboard with my analogy, but the point is this: somewhere deep inside you may be feeling your works will earn you heavenly rewards. You're not doing these jobs because you want to serve with joy; you're doing them out of fear that you're unacceptable if you don't. Your attitude is one of grudging service.

Here's a real divine permission for you: "For we conclude that a person is put right with God only through faith, and not by doing what the Law commands" (Rom. 3:28, GNT). It's not the doing that counts. It's the believing. If you're working because you choose to serve God joyfully and with faith that this is what God intends for you, then by all means, go ahead and work. But if you're working either *(a)* to make yourself look good (and others look bad) or *(b)* to ensure God notices how good you are, then you're missing the boat. Like Martha, you've allowed yourself to be worried and upset by many things while others have chosen "the better thing" (Luke 10:42, NCV). That thing is attitude.

I remember visiting in a church where one lone woman was slaving away in the kitchen during the coffee hour. I asked if she needed any help. "No, thank you," she said in a sharp tone. "You won't know where anything is." I left "Martha" alone. In another church I observed the same scenario, except the woman in the kitchen was singing along to some lively Christian music as she laid out cups and saucers. When I offered to help, she said, "Come on in. I could use another hand. Everyone else seems to be tied up elsewhere today." No recriminations, no "shoulding." She was being "Mary" in the kitchen.

## Permission to Be Selfish

We all know "saints." One lady I know whom most people would label saintly is always there for others. She's the first to visit the sick, the first to bake cookies for the church social hour, the first to volunteer to work at the senior citizens' drop-in center. You always receive a warm welcome at her house, and you can count on tea and home-baked goodies being served. She takes care of her grandchildren, supports a wayward grandson, and brought her aged mother-in-law to live with her. She's there for her children— willing to do whatever they need from cooking to babysitting, from sewing to gardening. Everyone knows they can count on her to say yes to any request. She never complains, never criticizes her family in any way or gives any indication that she would like to have some time for herself. Occasionally she might talk about a book she'd like to read if she had time or a place she'd like to visit if she could ever get away. Sounds like a woman whose price is far above rubies, doesn't she?

A few years ago, friends noticed she wasn't looking well. She had lost weight, was always tired, and appeared pale. However, she refused to go to the doctor. Instead, she continued as she always had; but now, obviously everything she did required more effort. Her family begged her to slow down; her friends remonstrated with her over her decision not to seek medical advice; her church prayed for her. Her husband tried to take over some of the chores, but she wouldn't let him. Her family tried to cut down on their usual demands, but she continued to supply them with food and labor. She dragged herself to church functions and visited in the hospital as she always had. We all worried about her but felt helpless to do anything.

Finally she collapsed, and finally she gave up being a saint.

You see, this lady had built her life on her saint persona. She didn't know how to be anyone else. She didn't know how to let others care for her, how to take time for herself, how to say no when she needed to, how to be a whole person with her own needs and wants. All she knew was that she should please others, and that "should" nearly killed her.

Now she had to let others take care of her. She had to let go of all her responsibilities, duties, and commitments. And we noticed subtle changes that suggested a much deeper change going on within. She began to use the "I" word—"I want some tea, please." "I'd like to go into town today." "I don't think I'll work at the church luncheon." She also began to do things just for herself without asking permission from others first. She'd take a whole afternoon and spend it reading a book. She'd go into town and shop for herself. She puttered in her garden, tending her flowers, not the vegetable patch.

She was learning to love herself first.

That's the divine permission you're given: to love yourself. Jesus told us that the second great commandment is to love your neighbor as yourself (Matt. 22:39). In other words, love yourself first and then love your neighbor just as much. Allowing others to walk all over you, to use and abuse you, to push you around and treat you like a servant is not loving yourself at all. In fact, it is negating the divine Spirit of God within you. It is saying you're not worthy of respect or love from others.

## Group Exercise

Read this passage from *The Velveteen Rabbit* together:

> "What is REAL?" asked the Rabbit one day, when they were lying side by side near the nursery fender, before Nana came to tidy the room. "Does it mean having things that buzz inside you and a stick-out handle?"
>
> "Real isn't how you are made," said the Skin Horse. "It's a thing that happens to you. When a child loves you for a long, long time, not just to play with, but REALLY loves you, then you become Real."
>
> "Does it hurt?" asked the Rabbit.
>
> "Sometimes," said the Skin Horse, for he was always truthful. "When you are Real you don't mind being hurt."
>
> "Does it happen all at once, like being wound up," he asked, "or bit by bit?"
>
> "It doesn't happen all at once," said the Skin Horse. "You become. It takes a long time. That's why it doesn't often happen to people who break easily, or have sharp edges, or who have to be carefully kept. Generally, by the time you are Real, most of your hair has been loved off, and your eyes drop out and you get loose in the joints and very shabby. But these things don't matter at all, because once you are Real you can't be ugly, except to people who don't understand." *

---

* Margery Williams, *The Velveteen Rabbit or How Toys Become Real* (New York: Bantam Doubleday Dell Publishing Group, 1922), 5, 8.

## Questions for Group Reflection or Private Reflection

1. How can you allow divine permission to influence your life?
2. Think about who will love you as you shed the "should's." Name those people and thank God for them.
3. Who might not understand the new freedom you experience? How could you respond to those persons?
4. How "real," in the sense described in *The Velveteen Rabbit*, do you feel right now?

## Prayerful Concerns

Lord Jesus, I want to sing my own song and dance my own dance to the tune you have created for me. Help me to let go of anything that binds me or holds me back from your grace and glory. In your name, I ask this. Amen.

## For Your Journal

Return to the page in your journal with the headings Should, Action, Permission, and Freedom. Under Permission, write the verse that gives you permission to avoid the "should's." Under Freedom, jot down your thoughts about the kind of freedom you now have. What will you do? What will you say? What will you have? Now make four lists:

1. What would you do if you knew you couldn't fail?
2. What would you do if you knew no one would be upset with you?
3. What would you do if you knew you could give up before completing if you chose to?
4. What would you do if you knew you could get emotionally involved and still be safe?

Consider what these lists say about how you're living your life today. Note your observations in your journal.

# Three Things to Do
# Before Reading the Next Chapter

1. Do one thing just for yourself. Do something you fear others may regard as selfish. You might buy yourself a special treat or take time for an activity only you enjoy doing.

2. Be like Tom Sawyer, who convinced others to paint a fence for him by acting as though it were a pleasurable thing to do. Choose one task you do not enjoy and see if you can convince yourself it is pleasurable. Find some aspect of it that you can count as a positive. Tell someone else about it.

3. Reflect in your journal on the following questions: What did you do just for yourself? Did you feel selfish? Did anyone else say it was a selfish act? What job did you manage to make pleasurable? What happened?

# 6
# Living in the Now

Who of you by worrying can add a single hour to his life?
—Matthew 6:27, NIV

During a visit to Hampton Court, Henry VIII's pleasure palace just outside London, England, I wandered away from the guided tour and ended up in the kitchens. These subterranean rooms far below the beautiful palace were dark, cold, and damp. I hurried though the nearest doorway to escape the gloom. As I stepped over the threshold, my foot caught on a depression in the stone. When I looked down, I saw it was the shape of a foot. *Why would the builders chisel a footprint into the stone step?* I wondered. Then I realized that the footstep hadn't been made by the builders but by hundreds and hundreds of people, each one stepping up, as I had, to leave the kitchen. Each footstep wore away the stone, like water dripping on a rock bed, until a perfect footprint was formed. I slipped off my shoe and put my foot into the depression. Instantly I was part of all those who had gone before me and all who would come after me. But I was also in the *now* of that moment.

Every part of our lives is like that experience: it is part of all that has gone before and of all that is yet to come, but it is separate. It is *now*.

I want to share with you the greatest secret to keeping close to God: *Live in the now.*

## Are You Living in the Past?

Many people miss the now because they are too caught up in looking to the past—looking at what was, who was, and how it was. It can be as simple as Mom's apple pie.

My husband and I were having dinner with good friends of ours. When our hostess served dessert, a wonderful-looking apple pie, her husband, George, remarked, "Ah, apple pie. Marcie makes a great apple pie. Of course, it's not as good as my mom's was. No one can make a pie the way my mom did."

The pie was fabulous, but George would never know. Convinced it couldn't be as good as mom's, he didn't really taste the treat in front of him. This is how a past experience can cloud and take away pleasure from a present one.

When I moved from the city to accept a job in the country, the children and I chose to live on a farm. We kept chickens and donkeys. Each day we needed to carry water for them to the barn, a good distance from the house. The first winter we were on the farm, in mid February, we had a blizzard warning. I brought up extra water and feed to the barn in anticipation of the storm to come. The blizzard hit hard and stayed for nearly three days.

When the snow finally stopped, I looked toward the barn. Drifts were piled up on the path—blown in behind a stand of small trees. In some places they were nearly over my head. My small snowblower was useless in the face of such high drifts. It took me a whole day of hard, back-breaking work to clear a narrow path the old-fashioned way—with a shovel.

One morning the following spring I was walking up to the barn on a perfect day: the sky was blue, the air was warm, the grass was green, and the birds were singing joyously in the trees. But I wasn't enjoying the perfect spring morning. My mind was elsewhere. I was already in the future, thinking about the past.

*This will all be covered by snow again. I'll have to clear the path again.* My past experience and my dread of the future took away the joy of the present moment.

We carry our past experiences into our interactions with other people. The old adage "once bitten, twice shy" seems to apply to our expectations of others. If you've had a bad church experience in the past—perhaps with a group who was not as welcoming as they might have been, a pastor who didn't listen to your story, or a holier-than-thou church member who made you feel less of a Christian—you may hold back from joining any church group, expecting every pastor to be a poor listener or to judge others and how they live out their faith. No wonder our church families can have such complicated relationships.

> *We carry our past experiences into our interactions with other people. The old adage "once bitten, twice shy" seems to apply to our expectations of others.*

For some people the past is just that—past. They have no trouble letting yesterday go and moving on with their lives. When I was a professional speaker, touring five cities in five days, I had to learn how to let yesterday go. Otherwise I found myself focusing on yesterday's audience, yesterday's mistakes, and yesterday's challenges and, in the process, shortchanging today's audience, who weren't receiving 100 percent of my attention.

## Are You Living in the Future?

What happens if you swing the other way and become too focused on the future? Are you one of those people who always look ahead, setting goals and making plans? You're not living in the now either. You're in tomorrow, next week, next month, next year. For you, today is temporary; it's not worth bothering about because tomorrow is all that really matters.

Your anticipated goal or plan may simply be an event. My son and his fiancée were engaged two years before the big day. For two years they lived in the future, planning, dreaming, and organizing the wedding. They were marking time, waiting for a future event. After the big day arrived and then passed, they both had difficulty adjusting to a life without a looming event.

A lot of us focus on a big day in our lives: a doctor's appointment, a job interview, a birthday, a move. That big day just keeps drawing our thoughts and attention, so that we miss the journey. It's hard to let the big day go and focus on the day we're in.

*People who continually live for the future often become disconnected from the present.*

People who continually live for the future often become disconnected from the present. In their daily life they refuse to settle in, put down roots, and make friends because they see now as a temporary spot on their journey to the future. I lived this way at one time. I'd taken a teaching job only because it was all I could get, and I planned to move on as soon as something better came along. I didn't get involved with any people or activities in the school and just marked time until I could move on. A year later I was still in the same job, and I'd missed a whole year of the now.

Maybe you're like Sleeping Beauty, waiting for her prince to come. You're waiting for some future event that will take you out of where you are right now. It could be getting a new job, sending the kids off to college, losing weight, winning the lottery, or retiring. Like Sleeping Beauty, you may find the brambles growing around your life.

I've met Christians who are waiting for some future event to make their lives full and rich. They're waiting until they're "good enough" to teach a Bible class, participate in Holy Communion, join the church. Over and over again, they miss out on the now by thinking God will truly accept and love them only when they reach a special plane of goodness. Not true!

A pastor once described a visit he made to someone who was dying. The parishioner told him, "First I was dying to finish high school and start college. Then I was dying to finish college and start work. Then I was dying for my children to grow old enough for school so I could go back to work. Then I was dying to retire. Now I'm just dying."

If you are focused anywhere but on this present moment, you are missing the only time you can be sure of experiencing. The past is gone. The future is unknown. Having tried to relive the past and to experience the future before it arrives, I have come to believe that in between these two extremes is peace.

## Learn to Live in Separate Compartments

Recently folks who bought a desk from us asked if we could deliver it to their home. Since we had a truck, we readily agreed. We found the house tucked away on an acre of land in a new sub-division. What a house! Four thousand square feet of fabulous space! The owners offered a tour of the house. They took us into room after room: a game room, a television room, a craft room, a sewing room, a child's room, a guest room, a great room, a living room, a dining room, and several rooms that were nameless. They couldn't possibly enjoy that fabulous house all at once; it could be enjoyed only room by room, in separate compartments.

Living in the now is like living in that house. It is living room by room, in separate compartments. Many people drag everything along with them all the time. When you go to work, do you bring along the worries, fears, doubts, and frustrations of your home life? Are these concerns with you, clouding what you do? When you go home at night, do you drag all the worries, fears, doubts, and frustrations from your job into your home?

To live in the now is to live in separate compartments. When you go to work, be completely focused on the job. Put all home thoughts away. It will be a continual, conscious putting away. When you catch yourself drifting back to home concerns, say to yourself, *I won't think about that now. I'll think about it when I get home.*

Do the same thing at home. Put work thoughts away in their own compartments. If you must bring actual work home with you, set aside a specific time and place (not in the family room where all the home-related action is) to do work-related activities.

You can do your worrying in a separate compartment too. In the movie *Gone with the Wind*, Scarlett O'Hara demonstrates this ability. At one point she says, "I can't think about that right now. If I do, I'll go crazy. I'll think about that tomorrow." She is worrying in a separate compartment. Matters that don't require worry today can wait until tomorrow. Scarlett isn't procrastinating—she understands how to compartmentalize her worries so that tomorrow's worry doesn't overshadow today's now.

My children found my method of compartmentalizing worries frustrating. They couldn't get me in a dither about an issue that needed an answer next month. I would mentally decide when I needed to make a decision and I'd say, "Don't ask me about that now. Ask me next Friday (or next week or next year)." I'd let it go and not worry about it until then. How did I do it? I kept reminding myself, "Therefore do not worry about tomorrow, for tomorrow will worry about itself. Each day has enough trouble of its own" (Matt. 6:34, NIV).

Likewise, you can compartmentalize trouble, grief, or sorrow so that you are still able to function in your world. When a dear friend of mine died suddenly and tragically in an accident, I was in the middle of a week of seminars. I felt overwhelmed by my grief, but I realized I had to get through the week and continue to give the seminar attendees what they deserved and expected. So I compartmentalized my grief. I put it away except for short periods when I could allow myself to mourn: on the road, in the evenings in my hotel room. The rest of the time I put my sorrow aside and got on with my job. When the week was finally over, I did mourn for my friend, but the excruciating pain was mitigated by my short times of grieving during the week.

You can cope by living in even smaller compartments. When you are going through severe emotional distress, compartmentalize that stress into small, manageable segments. When I was going through a painful divorce, I would lie in my bed at night and say to myself, *Can I trust God to be with me and hold me up for the next five minutes? Yes, I can.* And so I'd live for the next five minutes. When that time was up, I'd do it again. As the old adage says, "Life is hard by the yard, but inch by inch, it's a cinch!" When the going got really rough, I broke it down to one minute at a time.

That's what it means to live in separate compartments—to live moment by moment, letting the worries and issues of this moment be the only ones you consider. The worries and issues of the next moment can wait until then.

Here are some easy ways to bring yourself back into the now when you feel yourself slipping backward or forward or worrying needlessly about what doesn't need your attention right now.

### 1. Try "Stop, Look, Listen"

Do you remember the instructions you learned for crossing the street when you were a child? First you stop, then you look, and then you listen. Follow the same steps to enjoy the now moments in your life. Stop whatever you are doing. Now look around you. Don't just glance around; really look. Pretend you've never seen your surroundings before. Try to see every possible detail. Now close your eyes and listen. Really listen. Listen for the sounds around you from the loudest to the faintest. Sit quietly for a moment. Listen for the still small voice of the Spirit. You're in the now with your Lord.

## 2. Do One Thing at a Time

Typically in our society, we believe that time must be filled with as many activities as possible. We eat dinner while we watch television. We read a book while we ride a bus. We talk on the phone while we fold the laundry. On a lovely morning, we'll decide to sit on the deck and enjoy a cup of coffee, but we also take the radio, the television, a book, the newspaper, a laptop computer, some handwork, or the telephone. Or we might plan to catch up on bill paying, correspondence, mending, or the grocery list.

If we take only a cup of coffee, what happens? We find other things to do. We see the roses need pruning or the lawn needs mowing or the trash needs to be picked up. So we rush for our pruning shears, lawn mower, or trash can. The moment and the morning are lost.

Is it possible to do just one thing at a time? Try it for yourself. Take that cup of coffee and sit in a lawn chair. Taste the coffee— really *taste* it. When was the last time you really tasted something for itself? Now feel the lawn chair beneath you, the breeze on your face, the sun on your back. Hear the birds in the trees, the traffic on the road, and the children's voices from the next yard. Savor the moment completely. Experience the joy of the now.

## 3. Think of the Hourglass

Here's another way to experience the now. The sand in the top of an hourglass represents the time to come. The sand on the bottom represents the time that is past. The grains of sand pass through one at a time, just as our lives pass by one moment at a time—no more and no less. Whenever you find yourself dwelling on the past or projecting into the future, think of the hourglass and remind yourself, *One moment at a time.*

When you begin to live in the now, you'll begin to experience something called *flow*. What is flow? In baseball some hitters find flow when they perceive the ball as larger than life and moving in slow motion. Flow is that perfect date when time flies by. Flow is the words leaping from your fingertips onto the report pages. Flow is the prayer time that feels like a moment but lasts an hour. Flow is the sense of being completely involved in the now, so much so that time and space become irrelevant. For an athlete, specta-  tors disappear, and only the javelin, the ball, or the finish line is there. For the office worker, the report becomes central; no thought of coffee break, picking up groceries after work, or enjoying the week- end interrupts the current endeavor.

*When you begin to live in the now, you'll begin to experience something called flow.*

A few years ago Gerald and I bought some property. Much to our delight, we discovered a small stream on the land. One cold November day we arrived at the prop- erty about ten o'clock in the morning with the express purpose of exploring the stream. We found it blocked in many places, gone underground in others, and looped back on itself at several points. We dredged, dug, and moved rocks until eventually the stream flowed freely from one end of the land to the other. Suddenly it was dark and snow was falling. When I looked at my watch I was astounded to see it was nearly four o'clock. Hours had passed, but we'd had no sense of fatigue or hunger—or of time. We were in flow, completely engrossed and immersed in the task at hand.

Flow is *now*—no thoughts of the past, no worries for the future interrupt. For the Christian, flow is being one with God and the universe.

### Group Exercise
- Briefly share reflections on the previous chapter's "Things to Do" exercises.
- Try the "Stop, Look, Listen" technique together (page 77).

Then ask one another: What did you see in the room you had not noticed before? What sounds did you hear?

How long did the group remain quiet?

## Questions for Group Discussion or Private Reflection

1. Do any experiences from your past have a negative effect on your present life? If so and if you are willing, share one with the group. If you choose not to share the experience, reflect on it privately and think about how it impacts your life. How would your life be different if that experience had never happened?
2. Is an event looming in your life? How does it affect your day-to-day life right now?
3. Do you worry about something that may happen in the future? If you are willing, share it with the group. Why do you have trouble letting go of this worry, even though you know you can't do anything about it?
4. Have you ever had a "flow" experience? What happened?

## Prayer Concerns

Heavenly Father, I want to be in the now with you. I want to experience each moment as if it were the only moment in my life. Help me to do this. Remind me often that only this moment is of concern to me. Amen.

## For Your Journal

Write 2 Corinthians 5:17 in your journal. Then reflect on what this means to you in terms of letting go of the past.

Read Matthew 6:25-34. Write verse 34 in your journal. Reflect on what this verse means to you in terms of how you look at the future.

Write 2 Corinthians 6:2. Reflect on what this passage communicates to you about living in the now moments of your life.

# Three Things to Do Before Reading the Next Chapter

1. Choose a favorite food. Now sit down at the table and eat this food. Take one bite at a time. Chew slowly. Roll the food around in your mouth. Taste it fully. Avoid thinking about tasks to be done or looking around the room and wondering what you should be doing. Try to focus entirely on the eating experience. It's not as easy as it sounds!

2. Make a commitment to use "Stop, Look, Listen" once a day for the next five days. Try the exercise in unlikely places—on the commuter train, in an elevator, in the dentist's chair, in a restaurant, at the bus stop, at home while brushing your teeth. Be in the now in that moment—totally involved in every aspect of your surroundings. Savor the sights, sounds, smells, and tastes of the moment.

3. Reflect in your journal on the following questions: What favorite food did you choose to eat? How did this experience differ from the way you usually eat? What happened when you used the "Stop, Look, Listen" technique? What insights did you gain from this experience?

# 7

# Why Pray When You Can Take Pills and Worry?

We are often troubled, but not crushed; sometimes in doubt, but never in despair; there are many enemies, but we are never without a friend; and though badly hurt at times, we are not destroyed.

—2 Corinthians 4:8-9, GNT

*R*ecently I experienced a pretty bumpy ride on the commuter flight I regularly take. Across the aisle from me, a woman was engrossed in her work. Papers lay scattered across the seat next to her. She never even looked up as we bounced from air pocket to air pocket. In front of me, an older man, white-knuckled, moaned, "Oh my God. Oh my God," in a never-ending litany. Which person's stress was caused by the turbulence?

You might be tempted to say that the man was the one experiencing stress caused by the turbulence. In fact, the answer is neither passenger, because it wasn't turbulence that caused the stress; it was the reaction to the turbulence that caused the stress. You often see someone riding out one of life's more bumpy trips—illness, death, unemployment, relocation—with little sign of stress, while someone else faced with a similar challenge falls to pieces.

It's easy to see how this can happen if you picture life as a seesaw. On one end of the seesaw is a positive reaction to a situation; on the other end is a negative reaction. When you react positively, you feel strong, empowered, confident. When you react negatively (as the unhappy airline passenger did), you feel angry, worried, nervous, unhappy, powerless, and upset. It would be great if you could stay on the positive side of stress, but people react both ways, depending on the situation. That reality causes your life seesaw to shift up and down between feeling okay and feeling stressed out. Stress is an everyday fact of life. You can't avoid it.

*Stress is an everyday fact of life. You can't avoid it.*

Often we attribute a person's ability to deal with stress as a sign of how pious or holy he or she is. We think that really good Christians never have a seesaw that tilts to the negative, and if our seesaw gets stuck on the negative side, something must be wrong with our Christian walk.

What causes you to react—either positively or negatively? Here's the cruncher: everything! Everything in life is a stressor.

What is a stressor? A stressor is anything that requires you to react. Stressors can be people. I'm sure you can name a few people who cause you to react—positively or negatively. Stressors can be places, such as the dentist's office. Stressors can be situations, such as a meeting with your child's teacher. Events can be stressors: a big birthday, a wedding, a funeral. Stressors can be things as varied as an unexpected bill, weight gain, a phone call. People, places, situations, events, and things—all are stressors. You are continuously reacting and adapting to these stressors as they come into your life.

Whether you are experiencing major life changes or minor everyday hassles, your reaction to these stressors creates the stress response on your seesaw. The way you adapt or cope determines whether your seesaw tilts to the "feeling okay" side or the "feeling stressed out" side. You can't change the person, place, situation, event, or thing, but you *can* change how you react.

As Christians we have the most positive, powerful coping mechanism of all: prayer. So why do we end up being stressed out? Even though we know prayer offers the best way to deal with the people, places, situations, events, and things in our lives, if they're stressors that cause us to react negatively, for some reason, most of us try to deal with them by using various negative coping tactics first. For example:

**Denial**—pretending everything is just fine

**Overindulgence**—having that second scoop of ice cream or a whole pack of cookies when life gets tough

**Illness**—feeling bad ("Sorry, I have a headache.") or actually becoming sick (Have you noticed how often illness strikes when you're under stress?)

**Revenge**—planning to get even with the stressor (usually a person in this case)

**Tantrums**—stamping your feet and insisting on your way

**Withdrawal**—slamming the door and leaving the room or withdrawing emotionally from the situation

**Worrying**—fussing and fretting to the point of losing sleep and peace of mind

**Passivity**—giving in, becoming a doormat for your stressors

**Stubbornness**—digging in your heels and refusing to deal with the stressor

**Faultfinding**—blaming the whole mess on someone else

**Anger**—getting mad, either erupting on the surface or simmering inside, ready to blow up at the slightest aggravation

It would be nice to think that we Christians are above using such tactics with the stressors in our lives. But the truth is that we use all of them at one time or another. We usually have a favorite one that we pull out when faced with a person, place, situation, event, or thing that brings out a negative reaction. Then we hear others saying, "Oh, don't upset her; she will get in a huff and leave," or "Mom's in a snit again; she's not talking to anyone," or "You're wasting your breath; once he makes up his mind, he's not going to budge," or "It's easier to just go along with him; otherwise, he will start to yell and insist he's right," or "I can't get her to make a decision; she just says, 'Whatever you want to do . . .' It's so frustrating."

Personally, I go for the overindulgence tactic. When I'm upset, angry, or worried, I head for the refrigerator!

*When people, places, events, situations, and things don't meet our expectations, we tend to react negatively.*

One major stressor for many people is unmet expectations. You have expectations for so many aspects of your life. If you're a parent, do you remember holding that child in your arms for the first time? I do. I expected my child to grow up to be bright, intelligent, and helpful. What's more, I just knew that my child would never fuss over clothes, be a picky eater, or ever say the "f" word in public! What happened? The child grew up, and yes, fussed over clothes, fussed over food, and did indeed say that word in public. I sure experienced a lot of stress from unmet expectations related to my child!

When people, places, events, situations, and things don't meet our expectations, we tend to react negatively. Perhaps you can relate to some of these examples:

The new house has a leak.

It rains on the day of the carefully planned outdoor wedding.

Your friend forgot your birthday.

Yes, these are the little things in life that cause negative stress when we don't get what we expect. But what about expectations related to the outward signs of the Christian life?

The committee voted to paint the sanctuary light blue, and you wanted the beige.

The difficult person in the Bible study takes over the group.

The women's group is tied up with procedural wrangling.

Christian life is not what you expected. And what about life itself?

Your spouse is very ill.

Your son is disrespectful of you.

Your pastor disagrees with your views.

And the world?

Crime is on the increase.

Terrorism is a real threat.

Prices keep going up.

Morals keep going down.

Spiritually?

You feel out of touch with God.

Your prayer life doesn't have the power it once had.

Your daily walk has become dull and dry.

Where will it all end?

Are you feeling stressed just reading this? You're not alone. We seem beset on all sides—our inner spiritual life, our outer Christian life, our family, our society, our world. So, like many, we turn to negative coping mechanisms. We deny there's any problem at all. We try to withdraw from the world, shut ourselves up in our homes, and isolate ourselves from the problems around us. We worry more. Just look at the sales of antidepressants. We blame the whole mess on the government or the climate or the economy. We get mad; road rage is a good example. We overindulge to compensate, which is one reason so many people are grossly overweight. We plot revenge, form vigilante or militia groups. Or we say there's nothing we can do anyway and give up.

Is there a way to bypass these negative tactics and move directly to the power of prayer? Let me tell you how I do it.

My mother told me a beautiful analogy of how God takes care of us and everything around us. She told me to picture myself in the palm of God's open hand. If I am in God's palm, then all that happens to me on account of those stressors—whether people, places, events, situations, or other things—can only reach me through God's fingers. If God feels I cannot cope with one of these stressors, God's hand closes and keeps me safe inside. It's that simple. We live life in the palm of God's hand.

Picturing this, I can cope with whatever happens because I know God is with me. God knows what is happening and that I have the power within me to cope. Otherwise, God's fingers would have closed to shelter me.

How will I cope? With prayer—that is my only weapon. Even when I feel my prayer is unanswered or even unheard, I must continue to pray. I remind myself that "faith is being sure of what we hope for and certain of what we do not see" (Heb. 11:1, NIV).

## Group Exercise

- Briefly share reflections on the previous chapter's "Things to Do" exercise.
- When the going gets tough and stress builds, we need to remember what we are grateful for. The following exercise bring our "gratitudes" to mind. Hold out your hand. Each finger represents a specific gratitude. For each finger, go around the group once and share with one another what gratitude that finger brings to mind as follows:

1. *Little finger:* Share a place you remember, either now or in the past, that makes you feel relaxed and happy.
2. *Ring finger:* Share a smell that you like (such as fresh bread or roses).

3. *Middle finger:* Share a sound that you enjoy.
4. *Index finger:* Tell about a person who makes you feel good about yourself (or who made you feel good about yourself at some time).

Once everyone has shared these four simple gratitudes, sit quietly. Hold each finger one at a time; silently repeat the simple gratitude; then fold the finger into the palm of your hand. When all four fingers are folded into your palm, fold your thumb across the top. The thumb represents you, the person who holds these simple gratitudes within. Next, place your closed fist on your heart and silently thank God for what you have within yourself. These are simple gratitudes that no stressor can take from you. Use your gratitude fist when you feel yourself tipping toward the "feeling stressed out" side of your seesaw.

## Questions for Group Discussion or Private Reflection
1. Which negative coping mechanism(s) resonated with you?
2. In what ways do you use this tactic or tactics to deal with the stressors around you?
3. Name an unmet expectation in your life. How does it make you feel?
4. Why do you think God allows these stressors in your life? What can you do about them?

## Prayer Concerns
Loving Lord, thank you for keeping me so safe in the palm of your hand. Thank you for knowing what issues I need to face and what I can be sheltered from. Thank you for holding me so safe and secure throughout every moment of my life. Amen.

## For Your Journal
On a blank page, make four columns. Label them Stressor, Why, Usual Reaction, and Prayer Reaction.

*First column:* List stressors that cause you to react negatively right now—tipping your seesaw to the negative side. Think of the people in your life. Be specific—name names! Think of places where you feel uncomfortable, events and situations that cause you to worry, things that upset you. Pause and reflect on each stressor.

*Second column:* Why does this stressor cause you to react negatively? Do you feel threatened, angry, helpless? What is it about this particular stressor that pushes your hot button?

*Third column:* How do you usually deal with or respond to this stressor? Which coping tactic do you use with this stressor?

*Fourth column:* If you believe God knows this stressor is in your life and has given you the strength to deal with it, what can you pray? Write a brief prayer dealing with this stressor.

When you have completed the exercise, prayerfully read through the last column.

☼

## Three Things to Do Before Reading the Next Chapter

1. Use the gratitude fist the next time you feel stressed. It reminds you that God has given you simple things to be grateful for and that you are held in the palm of God's hand.

2. Consciously decide to pray about/for one of your stressors. Use the prayer from your journal and offer it at every opportunity.

3. Reflect in your journal on the following questions: Did you have an opportunity to use the gratitude fist? What happened? How did you feel? Are you praying about/for a particular stressor in your life? If the stressor is a person, have your prayers changed your attitude toward this person? How?

# 8
# Rollin' Down Life's Highway

All of you are Christ's body, and each one is a part of it.
—1 Corinthians 12:27, GNT

*M*y husband, Gerald, and I decided to go on a work-tour at the Anglican mission to Bequia in the Grenadines. We committed to three weeks with twelve people we'd never met before—traveling with them, living with them, eating with them, praying with them, playing with them. The situation reminded me of tour groups where strangers choose to travel and vacation together on a huge bus.

The experience was unsettling in some ways. Gerald and I are not joiners or "group people," preferring to do things on our own. But there we were—24/7 with strangers. Some were compatible; we laughed and joked and enjoyed one another's company. Some were a little off-the-wall; I was never too sure where they were coming from. Some were reserved; we knew no more about them at the end of three weeks than we had initially. And some were very open, sharing every aspect of their lives—in fact, perhaps more than we wanted to know ("too much information," as my son used to say). We learned how to relate to this disparate group of fellow travelers, but always in the back of our minds was the knowledge that it would be over in three weeks!

## Your Life Bus

Our journey through life is somewhat like being on a bus full of fellow travelers, only we've no idea how long the journey will last. Unlike a tour bus where the passengers remain the same for a whole trip, on our life bus some passengers get on and and off, while others travel the entire way with us. I heard another great analogy for this experience. Life is like being in a box of crayons: some of us are sharp, some are dull, some are pretty, some are fluorescent, and some have weird names, but we have to learn how to live in the same box!

What about your "life bus"? Who has traveled with you? Take a moment to think about

the friends you went to school with . . .
a next-door neighbor when you were growing up . . .
your favorite teacher . . .
a distant relative . . .
your coworkers . . .
your close family . . .
your church family members . . .
study group members . . .

The list of all the people who have shared your life bus over the years can be pretty amazing. Some are still on the bus with you. Some have gotten off, and some may get back on later. Some share your Christian experience. Some do not. Some ignore you. Some think it's their duty to tell you how to run your life. Some are your cheerleaders. Some are your strongest critics.

You may wish that some passengers would just get off the bus and out of your life! Our life buses aren't always filled with the most positive people in the world. There are a lot of folks taking up seats who seem bent on pulling you back from your walk with God. You may see them as your cross to bear, your burden, your sorrow, or your duty. Let me introduce you to a few of these passengers.

## Negative Noodles

My least favorite passenger on the life bus is the Negative Noodle, also called a Contrary Commentator. This person disagrees with everything you say or do. These folks dump negativity like a bucket of cold water on any ideas, thoughts, hopes, or dreams you may have. Negative Noodles seldom tell you why they disagree with you. They just do. Try sharing with them the idea you have for teaching a Sunday school lesson. "Oh, that'll never work! The kids will be bored! They only like video games," they say.

The trouble is, this negative attitude rubs off on you. You'll probably give up your idea. If you go ahead with it, you're just waiting for it to fail; and if it does, you could hear "I told you so," the Negative Noodle's favorite phrase.

After awhile you dread saying anything to these people. You find yourself avoiding conversations with them, holding back information, being secretive about your plans, keeping them in the dark about your ideas, and even lying on occasion! If your Negative Noodle is a close friend or even a spouse or parent, the relationship is never truly open and honest. How difficult that is for you! You probably spend a lot of time rationalizing the guilt you feel at cutting that person off from what's really important in your life.

## Helpless Hearts

Then there are the Helpless Hearts. These dear souls cling like ivy. As they lurch from crisis to crisis, they wait for someone, preferably you, to rescue them. The Helpless Hearts tell sad tales and pitiful stories. They pull at your heartstrings and sometimes even your purse strings. You spend a great deal of your time trying to assist them, bolster them up, and solve their problems. However, as soon as one problem is out of the way, another rears its head. If you volunteer to pray for them, they're quick to tell you that it never works!

## Steamrollers

The Steamrollers on your bus are determined to run your life—their way. They are out-and-out bullies, but they'll always tell you it's for your own good. "I hate to say this, but . . ."

They can see only one point of view—their own. You can recognize these people because they preface most of their statements with the words, "You should. . . ." Aah, fatal words. They really mean, *I don't expect you to; you'll probably fail;* or *if you don't, you'll feel guilty.* As I've said before, I call that being "should upon."

Jesus never "should upon" people. Jesus' statements were positive, present, action-oriented: "Love your neighbor," not "You should love your neighbor." Can you hear the difference in these statements? The first gives straightforward direction with no gray area: you either do it or not. However, that second statement leaves a lot of leeway, doesn't it? "Well, I tried to love my neighbor." Or, "Oh, I know I should, but he's such a difficult person."

Can't these negative people would change—or get off the bus?

## Cheerleaders

Sometimes we wish we could just ride the bus by ourselves, but we were created for fellowship, not isolation. Thank heavens we also have good, kind, positive people on our bus who are the cheerleaders of our life. They make our journey worthwhile. Consider these questions:

Who always upholds and encourages you?

Who is there for you in every circumstance?

Who urges you to reach for your dreams?

Who walks with you on your Christian journey?

These people are your cheerleaders, your earthly angels, the face of God in the midst of a despairing world. Spend time with them. Learn from them. Enjoy them. Talk to one or more of your cheering section at least once a day. Accept their outflowing to you. Enjoy the encouragement and nurturing they give to you. Make a habit of being aware of your cheering section, connecting with your cheering section, and allowing your cheering section to give you a boost of love every day.

## Folks You Don't Know

What about all those people on your bus you hardly know? Coworkers, people in your church, new neighbors, distant family members, the cashier at the supermarket, the mechanic who fixes your car—how do you relate to them?

As Christians we want others to hear the good news, yet most of us know a full-fledged "Are you saved?" can be a turnoff. How do we tell people on the bus about our faith without alienating them?

*As Christians we want others to hear the good news, yet most of us know a full-fledged "Are you saved?" can be a turnoff.*

You can begin with self-disclosure. Self-disclosure means opening up to other people—not throwing your whole life in front of them ("too much information" again) but letting them see you as a real person. Self-disclosure means allowing others glimpses of the person inside. This is always scary because you're never sure how they are going to react. You may feel vulnerable, fearful, or afraid. Will they laugh at you, use your disclosures against you, ignore you, or ridicule you?

They might, but in my experience, when I'm open and honest—not pretending to be someone I'm not—and avoid using holier-than-thou language, usually the other person reciprocates by opening up as well. When you look at the moon, you often see only a part of it, but you know it is much larger than it appears. When you converse with someone, you perceive only a sliver of the person's life; you may think that is all there is. Self-disclosure allows you get to know more about the whole person.

The big question is where to start. Well, for an easy first step, try adding a personal comment to your usual nondisclosure conversations. Comment on something you notice about the other person, something you feel about the day, something that gives you pleasure, or something that is worth noting. *Personal* is the key word here.

As I went through U.S. Customs on a trip from Canada recently, I noticed the customs officer's latex gloves. I said, "Those gloves look hot. They must be uncomfortable if you have to wear them all day." That's all. He stopped and looked at me in surprise. "They sure are," he said. I went on to observe how the world has changed, and that things like latex gloves are now a necessary protection. He responded with his thoughts about how the world is in a mess. I shared my belief that God cares for this world. For just a few minutes we connected in a real way—two strangers who shared the common bond of humanity.

*If we connect with others on a deeper level, we are able to show them the face of Jesus, if only briefly.*

A rose becomes beautiful and blesses others only when it opens up and blooms. If a rose stays a tight-closed bud, never fulfilling its potential, its beauty is lost. If we connect with others on a deeper level, we are able to show them the face of Jesus, if only briefly. If something in us draws them and causes them to want what we have, our job is done. If all Christians reflected the face of Jesus to others, our churches would be overflowing and our world would be closer to experiencing the reign of God.

Consider all the relationships you have with the fellow travelers on your life bus. You'll probably see that the relationships have changed over the years. Perhaps you have a sense of sadness as you realize that many relationships have faded. The special friend to whom you swore undying loyalty in grade school is now just a dim memory. The boss who stood by you through the rough shake-up in the office, the neighbor who shared your driveway and often shoveled it for you in the winter, great-aunt Mary who is now in a nursing home . . . somehow you've lost touch with them. There's an old saying: "Friendship is like money; it is easier made than kept." You may meet many people in your lifetime and make many acquaintances, but true friends are rare. Friends are earned, and once they're found, they must be treasured. Keeping a friend requires as much care as tending your garden.

When Robinson Crusoe was cast up on the shore of a tropical island, the lone survivor of a shipwreck, he had everything he needed for a comfortable life. He had more than adequate food, an ideal climate, and a beautiful setting. Though he was thankful for being alive, he cursed his solitary life. He said, "I am divided from mankind, a solitaire, one banished from human society. . . . I have no soul to speak to, or relieve me."* He was emotionally miserable because he was no longer part of the human fellowship.

Although you might prefer to travel alone on your life bus, that's just not how it works. We are put in fellowship with others, and our challenge is to learn how to relate to them meaningfully both for ourselves and for our fellow passengers.

**Group Exercise**
- Briefly share reflections on the previous chapter's "Things to Do" exercise.
- Write the following categories on four separate index cards or pieces of paper:
  Card #1: Cheerleader—Make a positive comment.
  Card #2: Negative Noodle—Say, "It won't work because . . ." (finish the sentence).
  Card #3: Steamroller—Say, "Don't be silly. You should . . ." (finish the sentence).

* Daniel Defoe, *Robinson Crusoe* (New York: Signet Classic, 1998), 63–64.

Card #4: Helpless Heart—Say, "Well, let me tell you my problem . . ." (make up a problem).

Hand the cards (or papers) to four people in your group. Go around the group and have each person (except the four people holding the cards) answer this question: *If you had complete freedom and enough money, and if everything you might worry about was taken care of, what would you like to do?* After each person answers, the four people with cards are to respond in their assigned role on that individual's life bus.

## Questions for Group Discussion or Private Reflection

1. How did you feel about the responses from the four people?
2. Which response bothered you most? Why? When have you encountered people who respond this way in real life ?
3. In reality, how do you handle people on your life bus who don't support you and your life choices?
4. Who are your cheerleaders? How do they make your life richer and fuller?

## Prayer Concerns

Almighty God, I know you are in control of my life bus. I also know that the other passengers are part of your plan for me. Help me show them your loving face. Amen.

## For Your Journal

*Note: You'll need colored pencils, crayons, or markers for this exercise. Plan to allot a little more time than usual to complete the entry.*

In your journal, draw a circle about the size of a half-dollar in the center of a page. Write your name inside the circle. Now think about the people with whom you have the strongest and closest bonds. Around the circle, draw more circles and write the names of these people inside—one name per circle. Begin to add circles for the people you care for, have warm feelings for, or are comfortable with. Continue adding circles for other people in your life—even those with whom you have a difficult relationship. Draw the circles and fill in the names quickly, as soon as they come to mind. Jog your memory by looking through your address book. Recall places you've lived and the friends you had there. Think of friends from work, school, political organizations, church congregations, study groups, clubs, and associations. Review each name and the experiences you have had with that person. When you finish, you'll have a picture of the traveling companions on your life bus.

Now think about the relationship represented by each circle. Either color the circle or draw around it with one or more of the colors using the following guide. Some circles may have several colors since relationships are complex.

**Red:** a difficult relationship—some tension, fear, worry, doubt, or anger exists between you and the other person.

**Orange:** a learning relationship—this person guide, teaches, mentors, or counsels you or fulfilled that role in the past.

**Green:** a growing relationship—you're aware that this relationship is still developing as you and the other person get to know each other and share your thoughts and feelings.

**Yellow:** a joyous relationship—your interaction with this person is characterized by fun, easy laughter, enjoyment.

**Purple:** an uneven relationship—one of you has more power over the other and uses it on occasion.

**Blue:** a relaxed relationship—you feel very comfortable with this person.

**Black:** a "dead" relationship—whether by choice, fate, or distance, this relationship is inactive.

Reflect on the people on your bus. On a separate journal page, write a short sentence about each circle on your life bus page. When you're finished, silently thank God for bringing these people into your life, remembering that each one has contributed to who you are today. Even if the influence was negative and hurtful, our loving, wise, and powerful God can bring good from it.

# Three Things to Do
# Before Reading the Next Chapter

1, 2.  Choose **two** of the following exercises:

    a.  Choose one of the yellow circles from your journal page. Set up a "play date" with that person. Do something you both enjoy. At the end of the time, thank this friend for being on your life bus with you. Self-disclose something you feel about your friendship.

    b.  Choose one of the circles colored orange from your journal page. Thank the person for his or her contribution to your life. Write a note, make a phone call, or, if the individual has passed away, say a prayer and thank God for bringing that person into your life.

    c.  Choose one of the red circles from your journal page. Reach out to that person in some way: a card, a phone call, or a visit. Be prepared to be rebuffed. Since this is a difficult relationship, the person may not react positively to your overture. However, in all difficult relationships, someone has to make the first move.

3.  Reflect in your journal on the following questions: What did you do with the person(s) you chose? How did the individual(s) react to you? What feelings did these exercises generate?

# 9
# Abundance and Outflowing

Keep your lives free from the love of money, and be satisfied with what you have. For God has said, "I will never
leave you; I will never abandon you."
                                    —Hebrews 13:5, GNT

Do you remember your first paycheck? I do. It was for a
week of work, and the grand total was $56.00. By the
standards of that day, I could do a lot with $56.00. Today
that paycheck would hardly pay for dinner and a movie. Money
just isn't what it used to be.

Money can cause more stress, unhappiness, arguments, and
anger than anything else. It's hard to walk with God when money
is on your mind!

Even so, money is important, whether we like it or not. We
live in a materially oriented society, and money symbolizes this
society. We may think Jesus didn't care about money, but we must
remember that the disciples had an accountant, Judas, the one
who handled the money and made sure their bills were paid.

Churches may think they don't care about money either. Yet
how many times have you winced at another appeal to your
generosity: the organ fund, the mission drive, the mortgage pay-
ment? Televangelists routinely ask for donations; the offering is

an integral part of the program. I remember being on a committee to invite an evangelist to speak to our church. "He lifts a good offering," one member said about a prospective invitee. It was easy to see where the priorities were. Giving often is regarded as a barometer of the health of the church.

You may not be comfortable with this discussion. Perhaps you are thinking, *Money is so crass! I'd rather discuss spiritual matters. I hate to even think about money. I have no control over it anyway. I don't know how to deal with money. I just leave it up to God.* A lot of us feel we have no real control over money; saying we've given the problem to God allows us to let go of the issue.

Some Christians believe we should not be concerned about money personally because Jesus told us specifically to be free from worrying about money:

> Therefore I tell you, do not worry about your life, what you will eat or drink; or about your body, what you will wear. Is not life more important than food, and the body more important than clothes? Look at the birds of the air; they do not sow or reap or store away in barns, and yet your heavenly Father feeds them. Are you not much more valuable than they?—Matthew 6:25-26, NIV

Many will tell you that they never think about their finances but just "trust in the Lord to provide." Or worse, they will tell you that you should be trusting in the Lord and not worrying about the bills piling up on your desk. In fact, some will infer that if you worry about money, you can't be much of a Christian!

Have you ever taken a hard look at your true feelings about money? Read the following list of phrases and jot down or say aloud the first completion of the sentence that comes to mind. Don't worry about what you're saying or why you're saying it. Just complete the sentence.

Money makes people . . .

Money equals . . .

If I had money, I'd . . .

Money causes . . .

In my family, money meant . . .

I'm afraid that if I had a lot of money, I would . . .

When I have money, I usually . . .

I think people who save money are . . .

Not having enough money is . . .

Money is important because . . .

Do your answers give you an idea of how you feel about money? Your attitudes and beliefs about money affect every area of your life. If your answers reflected negativity, you can expect that negativity to spill over. No wonder people often say that "money is the root of all evil."

What are some of your beliefs about money? When you talk about money, do you use metaphors such as "penny-pinching," "tightfisted," "money-grubbing"? When you say these words about money, you can feel the negativity being expressed. Do you believe you deserve to be prosperous, or do you believe you must scrimp and save in order to survive? What kind of role does money play in your life? Does the lack of or abundance of money play a leading role? Is money foremost in all your discussions and thoughts? Another attitude toward money says simply "more is better."

There are at least three typical ways of thinking about money that pit two extremes against each other—a good side and a bad side, so to speak.

Some people basically think about money in terms of abundance versus scarcity. That perspective tends to engender the feeling that there will never be enough money. No matter how much income grows, bills continue to pile up, and more money is required. On top of that assumption, many people believe deep inside that they're not good enough or capable enough to bring abundance into their life. Focusing on scarcity of money is called "poverty consciousness." The vicious cycle of believing there is never enough money distances people from the love of an all-encompassing God.

Another way of thinking about money pits "more is better" versus "less is better." This view always makes people, particularly Christians, feel uncomfortable. Can we face our beliefs honestly? We've heard the saying, "I've been poor, and I've been rich, and rich is better." But which is truly better: more or less?

*We can take a big leap forward in thinking about money when we realize money is neither good nor bad. Money is neutral.*

For one person, having little money results in freedom from worry about investments, possessions, and thieves. For another, having a lot of money results in freedom from worry about investments, possessions, and thieves! It's all in the perspective.

Yet another view is founded on the dichotomy of "money is good" versus "money is bad." Many believe that money itself and talk of money are unspiritual. In order to be a good person, money should not be a consideration in life. They hold up icons like Mother Teresa and say, "She didn't worry about money." No, she didn't, but her charity mission requires money in order to continue doing good works.

We can take a big leap forward in thinking about money when we realize money is neither good nor bad. Money is neutral. What is done with money may be bad or good: a dollar spent to buy drugs and a dollar spent to buy bread for a starving child are still each just a dollar.

In order to find your own truth about money, you need to sift through all you've heard and absorbed about money from parents, peers, church, and society. Only when you examine those assumptions can you move beyond money's hold over you. The bills and the debts won't go away, but the never-ending focus on having too little or too much; getting, hoarding, saving, spending, and so forth will go away. In its place will be a sense of sanctuary in the loving arms of God.

## An Abundant Universe

Try putting money in the context of a general belief about the universe we live in. Do you believe in an abundant universe? Some people claim that true wealth has nothing to do with money itself but is a belief in absolute abundance. When you read "absolute abundance," are you hit with mental images of poverty, crop failures, droughts, refugee camps, ghettos, and slums—places where people go to bed hungry and wake up hungry day after day? Do you think of that childhood admonition to eat all the food on your plate because children were starving in China? It's hard to believe that this is an abundant universe, yet many studies show that our earth has the capacity to sustain the life on it. The problem is not lack of abundance but unwise use of resources. God's world is an abundant one. That bounty shows itself over and over when we free ourselves from poverty consciousness and see the world as it really is:

Think of the night sky's billions of stars.

Think of fields ripe with harvest as far as the eye can see in the breadbaskets of this land.

Think of leaves upon the ground in autumn. Thousands upon thousands become nutrients for the soil, and the cycle continues.

Think of the ocean continually beating against the shore wave after wave, of tides rising and falling throughout the millennia.

Think of water flowing over a dam in seemingly endless supply, meadows full of flowers, skeins of geese overhead, a dandelion dispersing thousands of tiny seeds into the wind.

But don't stop. There are yet more forms of abundance. Abundance comes in the form of cultural and social enrichment. What enriches you? Music, beautiful art, fine pictures, books, friends, conversations, thoughts? There are so many experiences that make life richer and fuller.

What gives you joy? What brings that wonderful sense of being alive and thankful to be breathing on this earth? Sometimes it's as simple as a favorite cup to hold your morning coffee, a phone call from a friend, a letter, a plant on the windowsill, a special blanket, a smile from a coworker, a new baby, a sunset, a warm spring day, a hot shower, or a cold drink. Literally hundreds and hundreds of little things enrich your life and bring you joy. How rich you are! How abundant this world is!

*When you allow yourself to see the abundance all around you, it's easier to become part of that abundance.*

This is abundance. God created a world with more than enough for everybody, more than enough for you. When you allow yourself to see the abundance all around you, it's easier to become part of that abundance.

Truth be told, our world is a good, beautiful, nourishing place to be. What is evil is a belief that our world does not offer enough to go around, which leads to hoarding what we have in fear of losing it. For one moment, imagine how liberating this belief in an abundant universe would be. You would be free to share, to enjoy, to give, and to receive.

Money is part of this abundance. Not good money, not bad money—simply money. Not enough money, not too little money—just money. One of the best metaphors I know for abundance comes from the Bible: "'Test me in this,' says the LORD Almighty, 'and see if I will not throw open the floodgates of heaven and pour out so much blessing that you will not have room enough for it'" (Mal. 3:10, NIV). The King James Version wording is even more poignant. God promises to "open . . . the windows of heaven, and pour you out a blessing."

## Outflow to Others

If, despite the abundance promised to us, you believe the universe is not abundant, that there is not enough, you try to hold on to what you already have. You tighten up, keep things for yourself. You don't give. You don't outflow.

Instead of holding back, feeling penny-pinched, nervous about giving anything away, worrying about the bills, you can let it all go and believe that the windows of heaven are open for you. You can give as well as get. The injunction in Ecclesiastes to "cast your bread upon the waters" (11:1, NIV) tells you to let go of what you have and share it with others.

The more you give, the more capacity you have to receive God's abundance. You have to empty the glass before it can be refilled. Give and give again. Each time you outflow to another, you're essentially communicating that because abundance is promised, you can give it away, knowing more will always flow back to you.

> *The more you give, the more capacity you have to receive God's abundance. You have to empty the glass before it can be refilled.*

How do you outflow to others? It involves more than giving away money. Outflowing can take many forms— love, affection, appreciation, recognition, friendship, and caring. Someone coined the expression "random acts of kindness," and that's exactly what outflowing is. It tells the world you believe in an abundant universe and a loving, giving God.

As you go through your day, you'll discover many opportunities to perform random acts of kindness, to outflow to others, friends and strangers alike. You can outflow by giving time, words, touch, or some of your resources. You can encourage, teach, counsel. Smile at the overworked clerk in the bank. Offer to bring coffee to the switchboard operator. Drop an extra quarter in the tip jar at the newsstand. Bring cookies to the office. Send a card to a coworker. Call a cousin. Pay someone's car toll.

Thank the supermarket cashier. Compliment a stranger. Compliment the chef. Smile at a crying child. Offer to take the crying child. Send some flowers. Pick some flowers for someone else. Acknowledge a person with a smile. Put a quarter in an expired parking meter. Buy a gift for a friend. Each act is a simple way you can touch another's life.

> *You can outflow by giving time, words, touch, or some of your resources. You can encourage, teach, counsel.*

Can you imagine what a difference this kind of behavior—this outflowing—would make in your world? Imagine your church if you became an outflow of caring, creativity, helpfulness, kindness, and openness. That's what it's supposed to be like in a Christian church, but we know there are many sitting in the pews whose negative attitudes affect everyone around them. Because of that, everyone else holds back. But these folks need your outflowing the most. Someone has to be the first to outflow, and that someone can be you.

When one person begins to outflow, the practice spreads. It doesn't take much, I've noticed—positive comments, encouraging smiles, small gifts, thoughtful remembrances, genuine thank-yous. From the outflowing of self comes the outflowing of money. The purse strings loosen. Money is no longer the main topic of discussion at the church board meetings. People feel engaged and part of a truly loving community, and they want to contribute. Money gets to those in need, often anonymously, from someone who is outflowing from his or her own belief in an abundant universe.

At one point years ago I desperately needed money for a parking place in the city where I worked. My finances were so tight I could not squeeze out that extra cash. One evening I found an envelope in my mailbox. Inside was a hundred-dollar bill and a note: "The Spirit led me to give this to you; when you can, pass it on." It took some time, but when my finances improved, I prayed and anonymously passed on the hundred dollars with the same note. I often wonder how far that hundred dollars has gone, how many lives it has changed, and who has it today.

Basketball legend John Wooden once said, "You can't live a perfect day without doing something for someone who will never be able to repay you." In other words, much of our outflowing should be anonymous. We're not in it for the feeling of others "owing" us.

If you see your world as wonderfully, wildly abundant and begin to outflow some of that abundance, then your life will be abundant. As you give of yourself, love will flow back to you. That is the promise of the Christian faith.

*If you see your world as wonderfully, wildly abundant and begin to outflow some of that abundance, then your life will be abundant.*

## Group Exercise

- Briefly share reflections on the previous chapter's "Things to Do" exercises.
- You'll need one slip of paper for each person in the group. Have everyone write their name on a slip of paper and put it in a basket. Pass the basket around the group and instruct each person to draw out a slip. (If you draw your own name, you draw again). Keep secret the name you have drawn.

Sit quietly for a few moments. Then, write on the slip of paper a positive characteristic of that person. Make it specific and personal. Print your words so your handwriting will not be recognized.

Put the papers back into the basket. Pass it around again and this time each person takes the slip with his or her own name. Now each person in turn reads the positive description out loud to the rest of the group.

## Questions for Group Discussion or Private Reflection

1. How did you feel when you wrote a positive comment about another person in your group?
2. Would you have written anything different if your identity would be revealed?
3. How did you feel about receiving a positive comment?
4. Has anyone ever done something for you anonymously that made you feel loved and wanted? If so, how did you react?
5. What have you done for another person to outflow God's love? Did the other person know? How did the person respond to this act of love?

## Prayer Concerns

Bountiful Lord, thank you for the abundance in my life—for my home, my family, my friends, my community, my world. Thank you for all that you have given me, and most of all, thank you for the gift of your son, my Savior, Jesus Christ. Amen.

## For Your Journal

In your journal, make a list of people to whom you wish to outflow. Be specific. Say what you want to do and how you will do it. Set target dates to outflow.

## Three Things to Do
## Before Reading the Next Chapter

1. Give money anonymously to someone who needs it. Don't enclose a card or anything that might identify you. Just outflow. The amount isn't important—the outflowing is.

2. Outflow to yourself. Give yourself a gift of time by setting aside an hour to read, walk, sleep, pray, or simply do nothing. Remind yourself that time is one of God's abundant gifts to us.

3. Reflect in your journal on the following questions: What did you do in the time you gave yourself? How did it feel? Did anyone react to your taking time for yourself? How? What did you do for someone else? What was the result?

# 10
# Paint-by-Number Living

In view of all this, what can we say? If God is for us, who
can be against us?

—Romans 8:31, GNT

I had the privilege of hearing the wonderful speaker and
writer Denis Waitley describe living life to its fullest. He
illustrated his point with an analogy that struck a chord
within me. He said many people live as though life were a paint-
by-number picture.

For these people, life's picture has been determined for them,
and the colors already chosen. Everybody has little pots of paint
marked 1, 2, 3, 4, and so on, and a small paintbrush for each pot.
They look at the spaces in life marked "1" and carefully put their
number 1 paintbrush into the number 1 pot of paint. Then, just
as carefully, they color the small space, conscientiously staying
within the lines. Years later, when the picture is finally finished,
they look at it and say, "That's not what I wanted!" Often it's too
late to start again. Some die before they paint in all the spaces and
never see the completed picture.

Then Denis introduced a powerful metaphor. He said, "Imagine that your life is a big barn. A huge, wonderful barn. What I
want you to do is get big buckets of paint in all the colors you like

best, and I want you to get big, fat paintbrushes and splash paint on the barn of your life. Don't worry about what it looks like. Just use the color and designs and patterns that feel right to you."

What an incredible metaphor—splashing paint on the barns of our lives. To live life fully and exuberantly, choosing colors that reflect who we are, painting pictures that are just for ourselves. It's a vivid image—making big, wide swaths of living color on the barn, each color lovingly chosen and joyously applied.

It's a risk, isn't it? Maybe you'll choose colors that clash. Or perhaps the picture won't be as good as you hoped. Others may laugh at your color choices, belittle your painting efforts, or insist that you paint the barn their way.

## Imagining Dragons

Did you know that we have dragons in our lives? They're not the big, fire-breathing variety that pop up in numerous children's stories but secret little dragons who lurk in the corners of our mind. Most of the time, we're not even aware they're there.

I call them the What-If dragons. If you want to see them in action, just begin to think about splashing paint around in your life. Those What-If dragons will grow to paralyzing size, their fire-breathing power burning up any ideas you have about leaving behind a paint-by-number existence. It's hard to believe that something as small as a "what if" could change your mind, but when that "what if" becomes a powerful negative force that terrifies you into submission, a dragon of such proportions that you tuck your tail between your legs and go back to paint-by-number living, then the Enemy has won, and the joyful life we are promised becomes a might-have-been.

Often the What-If dragon that prevents us from taking risks is the one that whispers, "What if you fail?"

I've belonged to a lot of writers groups over the years. Getting together and letting others hear your work and offer helpful suggestions makes the writing business a little less lonely. In every group, there are always those who like to write but have never submitted anything for publication. They couldn't bear to risk rejection by an editor. Rather than risk failure, they do nothing. How sad. They'll never know if they could be the next John Grisham or Agatha Christie.

Would Jesus have ever begun his work if he had heeded this particular dragon? Would he have left his work, his home and family, and set out on his lonely three-year odyssey to bring the Good News to his Father's people?

What would you do if you knew you couldn't fail? Would you learn a new language, start a Bible study group, write an article for some publication, try for a promotion, read the lesson in the Sunday service? If you knew you couldn't fail, how many new risks would you be willing to take?

There's another What-If dragon lurking in our mind, just waiting to discourage us from doing any serious paint-splashing. This dragon whispers, "What if you break the rules?" By rules, I don't mean the legal laws of our land but The Rules—the hundreds of unwritten rules that govern our behavior and our lives.

Do you remember your first day in preschool or perhaps kindergarten, when the teacher gave you a picture to color and a big box of crayons? "That's your picture," she told you. "You can color it anyway you want." You grabbed a big green crayon and started coloring the sky. "Oh, no," the teacher said, taking the green crayon from you and handing you a blue crayon. "The sky isn't green; it's blue."

You just learned how the rules work. You can do anything you want—as long as you obey the rules. So you took the blue crayon and started to color. It wasn't as much fun, because now you had to think about what the right colors were to use on your picture. But you got back into the swing of things and began boldly coloring that picture.

Again the teacher stopped you. "Stay within the lines," she told you. "The lines are our friends."

Now you had to choose the right color and color within the lines that someone else had decided for you. It wasn't any fun, but you persevered.

The teacher came by again. Picking up your picture and showing it to the rest of the class, she said, "Look at this lovely picture! See how neatly it has been colored. And look at all the pretty colors."

Aah—now you understood. Choose the right colors, stay within the lines, and you will be praised by others, even held up as a good example.

So what happens when you're faced with an opportunity that doesn't fall within the rules?

> I think Jesus is our best example of someone who colored outside the lines. How often he upset the authorities of the day by breaking the rules.

I think Jesus is our best example of someone who colored outside the lines. How often he upset the authorities of the day by breaking the rules. He healed on the sabbath, ate with the tax-collector, spoke to the Samaritan woman, forgave sins.

What would you do if it didn't matter that you broke the rules? Would you learn a nontraditional trade? Would you apologize first, even if you were right? Would you turn down a promotion to spend more time with your family? Would you attend a conference where everyone else would be better educated than you? Would you speak up at a meeting?

One of the most insidious What-If dragons is the one who pretends to espouse a Christian virtue and thus dissuades you from taking a risk that is just for you and you alone. "What if you're being selfish?"

Oh dear. We can talk ourselves out of so many opportunities by telling ourselves it would be selfish of us to pursue them. It's

January as I'm writing this, and I'm sitting on the lanai of a condo in Florida. A friend of mine who owns the condo offered me a week here if I wanted it. Wow! But . . . the airfare would be costly. I'd have to leave my family behind. My husband would have to care for our pets and our home in Nova Scotia. My little dog would miss me. We're getting ready to move, and there's so much packing to do. The list is endless. All good reasons why choosing to be here seems selfish.

Yet I'm here. Why? Because I knew I needed these few days by myself to finish this manuscript. However, you can be sure that some people let it be known that they considered it pretty selfish of me to come here on my own. It's tough when others play the role of the What-If dragon.

If you could do something without anyone (not even you) thinking it was selfish, what would you do? Would you go back to school and arrange for child care several evenings a week? Would you ask to be taken off the overtime list even though the extra money is welcome? Would you take time each morning for devotions and let the family figure out how to pour their own cereal from the box?

If only we could let go, splash the paint of our lives, and see what wonderful designs God has for us!

## Reasons We Don't Splash Paint

Even if you don't have any What-If dragons lurking in the closets of your mind, you may still hold back from the risks of painting your own barn.

Are you feeling frustrated as you read this? Perhaps you are thinking, *Well, sometimes there are good reasons to avoid any risks.* Maybe they're not so much good reasons as good excuses. Consider the following four excuses to avoid splashing paint.

## 1. "I'm too old."

Question: Do you know how old you'll be by the time you learn to play the piano, fly a plane, volunteer in Africa, become a nurse, climb a mountain, train as a missionary, or . . . (insert your secret desire here)? Answer: the same age you'll be if you don't.

Our world has been set up so that certain ages are deemed appropriate for certain activities. You're supposed to go to school, have a career, retire, and die—in that order. If you buck the trend, you'll have a lot of people lining up to tell you you're being silly: you're "too old" to go back to school for your degree, travel to a missionary field in Africa, or learn to ski.

"I'm too old to . . ." is a perfectly good excuse you may use to avoid all kinds of risk taking in your life. But do you hear the sadness in those words? I honestly believe no one is ever too old to do anything he or she wishes to do. One of the greatest stories I've heard recounts how a woman at eighty years of age decided she wanted to climb a mountain. At age ninety-two, she is still climbing mountains.

## 2. "I've never done that before."

This is what I call rearview-mirror driving. It's like driving the car of your life by looking only in the rearview mirror. You don't know where you're going; you only look at where you've been. If you haven't been there before, you don't want to go!

This excuse lets you turn down all kinds of risks: speaking in public, writing for a newsletter, leading a group, joining a helpline, organizing a meeting.

## 3. "I have to be sensible."

The most wonderful risks that pop up in your life require not being sensible, going beyond where you are right now into areas you've never been before. Where would the *Star Trek* crew of the *Enterprise* be if they hadn't gone where no one had gone before? You may want to do things that look foolish to other people, but these adventures enrich, nourish, and create a sense of excellence in your life.

When I left my dull, albeit safe, job in the city to accept a less secure job in the country, my friends and coworkers were horrified. "You must be sensible," they told me.

Says who? Who says you have to be sensible? Where is it carved in stone that everything you do in life must be sensible? Where does the joy in your life go if you are busy being sensible? Where do the moments of wonder go? The excitement? They all disappear when you tell yourself, "I have to be sensible." We've been told that the things we do will look foolish in the eyes of the world. God doesn't ask us to be sensible.

### 4. "The timing isn't right."

Timing. What a great way to avoid risks. Simply blame your reluctance on the timing.

The timing is always right because the only time you have is this moment. If you wait until the timing is right, you may not be here. Or the chance may not be available anymore. The opportunity or chance may never occur again.

Instead, we say, "I'll wait until . . ." I'll wait until the kids have left home, until I get that raise in pay, until I've lost twenty pounds, until I get married, until I retire, until I win the lottery.

I wonder how different the world would be if Jesus had decided to wait until the timing was right. Perhaps he would have waited until the Romans left the land, the Pharisees lost their power, or his father no longer needed his help around the carpenter's shop.

It's hard to imagine the kind of freedom that splashing paint brings to mind. The paint-by-number picture is so much easier—and safer—than that great big barn waiting for us to open up the paint cans. But how sad to come to the end of our days and look back with regret, wondering how it might have been if we'd opened our lives to the leading of the Spirit.

I am convinced that it is God who has given us the barn and the Spirit who whispers the colors to use, who encourages us to paint with broad strokes, to be bold, to put aside our fears and doubts, and to paint with joy and exuberance.

## Group Exercises

- Briefly share reflections on the previous chapter's "Things to Do" exercises.
- Ask the group members to close their eyes while someone reads the following paragraph aloud:

Imagine you are walking down a country lane with a large field on one side. You see an old barn in the field. It's a large barn weathered and beaten by the elements. The shingles are gray and faded; the tin roof is rusty; the windows are broken and dirty. Now imagine that this barn is your life. You can do anything you want with it. What will you do?

After a few minutes of silence for imagining, invite people to share with one another their dreams for the barn.

## Questions for Group Discussion or Private Reflection

1. Which What-If dragon do you recognize in your own life? How can you tell it's there?
2. What excuse(s) do you use to avoid making any changes, splashing any paint, or taking any risks? Which seem to be your favorites?
3. What would you do if you knew you couldn't fail?
4. What would you do if breaking the rules didn't matter?
5. What would you do if you could do it without anyone (not even you) thinking it was selfish?

## Prayerful Concerns

Dear Lord Jesus, I'd like to paint my barn. Give me the courage to choose colors that give me joy, the freedom to paint boldly, and the wisdom to listen to my own heart. Thank you. Amen.

## For Your Journal

How do you recognize a What-If dragon lurking within you? Write down five things you would like to risk—opportunities, desires, dreams, wishes, possibilities, chances—any five. Look at each one separately and ask yourself this question: *What is preventing me from taking this risk?*

Write down your answers, no matter how silly or how trivial they may sound. Then look at them closely. Are they variations of one of these What-If dragons:

What if I fail?
What if I break the rules?
What if I'm being selfish?

Or are they "good" excuses like these?

I'm too old.
The timing isn't right.
I've never done this before.
I have to be sensible.

☼

# Three Things to Do
# Before Reading the Next Chapter

1. Think about the unwritten rules in your life. Break one of them. See
   how you feel about it. It doesn't have to be a big issue. For example, I went to a restaurant and ate dessert first. Then I had a main
   course. I broke the unwritten rule that says you must eat your veg-
   gies before you can have dessert.

2. If you can, attend a meeting, group, exhibition, party, class, lecture,
   play, movie, or other event that you would not ordinarily think of
   going to. Go with an open mind and see what happens.

3. Reflect in your journal on the following questions: What rule did
   you break? What happened? How did you feel? Did anyone else
   react? How? What function did you attend? What was the experience like for you?

# 11
# Lilying Around

Don't worry about anything, but in all your prayers ask God for what you need, always asking . . . with a thankful heart. And God's peace, which is far beyond human understanding, will keep your hearts and minds safe in union with Christ Jesus.

—Philippians 4:6-7, GNT

We all have goals. For most of us, just to *have* is a goal. For example, I want to *have* a big house on the ocean with sixteen rooms and a private study of my own and a three-car garage; I want to *have* my name in lights on Broadway; I want to *have* a family and a home life; I want to *have* the freedom of early retirement; I want to *have* the security of money in a savings account; I want to *have* a large church.

From there our goals move on to *doing* goals. In order to have things, we know we must do things. For example, I want to own my own company and be my own boss; I want to star in a Broadway musical; I want to meet a good person, get married, and settle down; I want to retire at age fifty-five; I want to invest my money wisely; I want to inspire people around me.

From *having* and *doing* goals we narrow down to goals about what we want to *be*. For example: I want to be successful in business; I want to be a great actor; I want to be a wife and mother; I want to be a free spirit; I want to be rich; I want to be an inspirational speaker.

That's the way we set goals in our world. We determine what we want to have. Then we work out what we need to do in order to have those things, and finally, what we will be when we've done it all and have it all. *Having. Doing. Being.*

## Live Like a Lily

In the world of the Spirit, God's world, the order is reversed. First we must decide what it is God is calling us to *be*. From that point we can begin to glimpse what we need to do in order to be that kind of person. Then and only then will the end result be what we have. Once we are *being* God's purpose for us, we can begin *doing*; and when we are doing, we are most able to enjoy *having*.

For example, do you want to inspire others? What would you need to do? Openly profess your faith; speak confidently about God's love; live so that others will see the face of God in your life. If you are a pastor who dreams of having a great congregation, you will realize your dream by doing what is required to be an inspirational person.

Let's look at some everyday *having* goals. After all, we're talking about real life, and having is part of that life. Perhaps you want to have a loving relationship with someone. You've tried want ads, social clubs, online groups, and so far nothing has happened. What if you asked yourself what kind of person you would need to be in order to have that loving relationship?

Perhaps you'd like to have the security of wisely invested funds. You leap into doing things—getting involved with various brokers, reading everything you can find on investing, putting your money into the market. Now you expect to *be* secure. But is security really guaranteed? Suppose you start at the other end of the goal. What is God calling you to *be* in relationship to your money?

To *be* faithful in tithing? To *be* generous to others who have less? To *be* honest in all your financial dealings? The Bible promises that when you are being this way, God will take care of you.

How do you concentrate on just being? I have found this the most difficult concept to grasp in my life. I was used to thinking about *doing*. I knew exactly what I wanted to do. I had no trouble thinking about *having*. I could make up a wish list at the drop of a hat. But *being*—that didn't sound like a practical way to live my life as a Christian.

Oh but it is! *Being* is what life's all about. You just have to learn how to live like a lily. Jesus said, "See how the lilies of the field grow. They do not labor or spin. Yet I tell you that not even Solomon in all his splendor was dressed like one of these. …Seek first [God's] kingdom and . . . righteousness, and all these things will be given to you as well" (Matt. 6:28-33, NIV).

> Being *is what life's all about. You just have to learn how to live like a lily.*

Pretty straightforward, isn't it? All you're asked to do is to be. Just as the lilies spend their lives simply being lilies—not petunias or turnips—so also you are asked to spend your life simply being you—not anyone else.

Perhaps you made paper snowflakes in school. You carefully followed the teacher's instructions, folding and refolding a square of paper. Then you took your scissors and began to snip, snip, snip along all the edges. If you were like me, you couldn't imagine that this folded piece of paper with all these bits cut out of it could ever become anything but a pile of paper scraps. Then you were told to unfold the paper.

Do you remember the awe, the wonder, the amazement you felt when you found a beautiful, sculpted paper snowflake in your hand? Even more, do you remember how amazing it was that no one else in your group had a snowflake like yours? It was a little miracle.

You are the same kind of miracle. You are one of a kind. There is no person exactly like you; even twins are not exactly the same. You are unique. You are you, and you are the only person who can be you. No one else is living life exactly the way you are living it. This is such an incredible concept. You are the only you!

*When you concentrate on being rather than on doing or having, you will discover you are living the life God has called you to live.*

That concept is the crux of *being*. All you need to do in order to be is learn how to be you. It may seem a simplistic way of looking at things, but no one else in this world can be you or live your life. Every moment of every day, if you are simply being you, the person God created you to be, you are moving in the right direction. When you concentrate on being rather than on doing or having, you will discover you are living the life God has called you to live.

## Expect Synchronicity in Your Life

Once you let go of all the stuff that fills your mind—wants, needs, goals, yearnings, desires—and simply be, you can begin to expect something called *synchronicity* in your life. Carl Jung coined this word. It means happenstance, coincidence, serendipity. I call it God-incidence. Suddenly those things you thought you might like to have or do begin to come into your life in unusual ways. A teacher of mine, a Quaker named Miss Parker, called it an unfolding. When she was waiting for an answer from God, she'd say, "I'm waiting for an unfolding." It's synchronicity.

Synchronicity happens to you all the time. Have you ever noticed that after you spend weeks looking at new cars and finally settle on a particular model, you then see that model everywhere you look? Where were they yesterday?

Synchronicity occurs in our lives over and over again when we stop striving and pushing for whatever we want to have or do. Instead, we let go of those desires, trusting God, who clothes the lilies, will take care of us. And God will honor our being by bring to us the abundant life we have been promised.

## Give God Your Dreams

I once attended a Christian visioning workshop where I was introduced to talismans and treasure maps. At the time, I thought the ideas were a little off-the-wall and worried that they smacked of the New Age movement. However, I trusted the instructors, two mature Christians who were strong in the faith.

We started by finding talismans for our lives. A talisman is a concrete symbol of your innermost wishes or desires. For example, if you've dreamed of living on a ranch and working with horses (having and doing), a small statuette of a horse becomes a talisman. A talisman for my dream of living on or near the water was a shell on my desk. A talisman is a small reminder that your life is in God's hand.

You may have heard about the tradition of Native American medicine bundles. A medicine bundle might contain an unusual rock, strand of hair, feather, bird's beak, animal skin, sweet grass, and other small objects with special meaning to the owner. The bundle of objects represents a person's spiritual life, and the owner believes it holds protective and healing power. As the owner grows older, more items are added. Medicine bundles may be buried with the owner or passed on to a friend. A medicine bundle is a collection of talismans.

At a Christian women's conference, a First Nations (Native American) woman led us through a dawn ceremony. She first unwrapped a roll of red cloth and explained that this medicine bundle reminded her of God's goodness and grace in her life. Each item held special significance and was precious to her.

Recently I learned that my father (who left my mother and me when I was nine years old) was of Native American descent. I investigated further and was surprised to discover that I was eligible for Métis status (a Métis is a person of mixed Native American descent) even though I was born in England and have red hair and blue eyes. It is the bloodline that counts, the elder told me, not the appearance.

Since I learned about this heritage, I have constructed a medicine bundle for myself, including these items:

- a small pouch of tobacco presented to me ten years ago when I spoke to a First Nations group in Western Ontario;
- a small, dark, flat oval stone with a jagged white line around one end, which reminds me of the crown of thorns my Savior wore on the cross;
- a fossil clamshell I found on a beach near our cottage when the kids were small.

There are other talismans that are special to me alone and shared only with God.

Talismans are tangible tokens you can touch, see, and hold. They continually remind you that God knows your hopes and dreams. God wants to give you your heart's desire because God loves you. "Delight yourself in the LORD and he will give you the desires of your heart" (Ps. 37:4, NIV).

And here's where this being, doing, and having business gets interesting. As I said earlier, we all know what we want to have. We probably have an idea of what we need to do in order to have it. But the Christian way says that the doing and the having are not what is important—being is.

So what are we supposed to be—our whole unique self? And how do we go about being that? The answer is in two scriptures quoted in this chapter:

Seek first [God's] kingdom and . . . righteousness.—Matthew 6:33, NIV

Delight yourself in the LORD.—Psalm 37:4, NIV

In other words, "lilying."

When we are fully engaged in seeking God and delighting ourselves in God's presence, all else falls by the wayside. Our striving and yearning, trying and hoping, reaching and dreaming—all lose their importance in our lives. We reach a state of peace with our lot and who we are. We become true children of God, living only to seek God's will and to worship God's glory.

When we are "lilying"—simply being a child of God—that's the time God fulfills the promise to give us the desires of our hearts. The talisman that we've kept as a reminder to let go and let God take care of our dreams becomes a reality in our lives. When we begin to *be*, God begins to work in and through us.

## Group Exercises

- Briefly share reflections on the previous chapter's "Things to Do" exercises.
- You'll need scissors and paper to make snowflakes. Fold a sheet of paper in half. Fold it in half again. Then fold it diagonally from corner to corner. (Someone is bound to remember how to do this!) Round off the open edges with the scissors and start snipping. Unfold your snowflakes and show one another.

## Questions for Group Discussion or Personal Reflection

1. Do you feel unique? Why or why not?
2. What do you think you bring to this group that no one else does?
3. What are some ways you can begin to simply *be*? How can you seek the kingdom of God? What would it mean to delight yourself in the Lord?
4. Do you believe God really has any interest in our goals and

dreams? Why would God care about something so personal and perhaps, material?

## Prayerful Concerns

Loving Creator, help me in my desire to be what you have called me to be. Help me to discover the person you have created as individual and unique as a snowflake. Amen.

## Journal Exercise

You will need some magazines, glue or tape, scissors, and colored construction paper. You're going to construct a treasure map. Here's how to do it.

In the middle of a blank journal page, write your name and draw a circle around it. Now, go through magazines, newspapers, or any other printed material. Let your eyes scan the words and pictures but don't see them in the context of the page—just as random words and pictures. Here's the fun part: as a word or a picture or a shape jumps out at you, or speaks to you, cut it out and paste it randomly on your page. Don't try to make nice, neat patterns. Just let it happen.

You'll know when you're done. At that point you'll no longer see inviting words or pictures to cut out. You now have a treasure map that has meaning to your inner spirit.

Take some time to examine this treasure map for any connections among the images and words. Are there surprises? Do any of your deepest desires appear in the map?

It's been said that we draw to us what we think about. As your spirit thinks about your treasure map images, it will draw to it the circumstances that support these images. God-incidences, unfoldings, synchronicities—expect them in your life.

# Three Things to Do
## Before Reading the Next Chapter

1. Find a talisman for your life. Notice what you dream about and yearn for. Then choose a talisman—something tangible that would best represent your dream. Put it where you can see it every day.

2. Devote some time to "lilying." Put away all your worries, hopes, fears, and doubts and sit quietly, reveling in the loving presence of God. Try to do this several times over the next few days. How long you spend lilying doesn't matter: two minutes or two hours. It's the lilying that matters.

3. Reflect in your journal on the following questions: What talisman did you find? Why did you choose it? Did you experience "lilying"? What happened? How has it changed your walk with God?

# 12
# Glimpses of God

This is how we know that [God] lives in us: We know it
by the Spirit he gave us.

—1 John 3:24, NIV

When my husband and I were planning to build a house, I
devoured all the design books I could find. That's how I
first found out about something called Zen windows. The
concept is that rather than having only large windows, a house
design would include small windows positioned so that a view is
glimpsed briefly, perhaps as someone comes down the stairs or
crosses a room. These Zen windows capture a vista in small, perfect previews before the whole scene is revealed.

We tried this design idea with a small window at the bottom
of our stairs, facing west. I called it the sunset window. Through it
we could see a glimpse of brilliant red sky, a branch of the maple
tree limned in gold, an edge of the barn outlined in golden rays—
a preview of the panoramic sunset that awaited us outside. We
need small "windows" in our daily lives that offer glimpses of God
as we go about the routines of work, home, and play.

Without such glimpses, we struggle on, feeling alone as our
feet stumble along the path and our hearts falter at what lies
ahead. Why is it so much easier to glimpse God when we are in

church or in deep prayer than it is to see God around us in daily life? When we're "out there," facing a shaky relationship or a tough problem in the workplace, why does God often seem so far away? Why does God often seem close when we're praying for a person but far away when we're dealing with that person face-to-face?

Perhaps it's because we don't know how to glimpse God in our daily life. It's a little like bird-watching. If you ever go out in the woods with serious bird-watchers, you'll notice that they seem to look out of the corner of their eyes for that special bird. Catching glimpses of God requires seeing God obliquely, not head-on, as Moses experienced at the burning bush.

*Our daily glimpses of God are there for us to enjoy. We just don't see them.*

Our daily glimpses of God are there for us to enjoy. We just don't see them. On my desk sits a pen with the words "This pen may be worth $20,000" written on it. Underneath are the numbers 6893-9874—nothing more. I no longer remember where the pen came from. I don't know what company gave it to me. I don't know what the numbers mean. I don't know where the $20,000 is. That pen may be worth $20,000 but not to me. Why? Because I don't know how to collect the prize.

A lot of Christians are in the same boat. We know we have the tool to help us walk with God, but we don't know how to use it. That tool is the Holy Spirit, who breathes spiritual power into our life. This personal Spirit enables us to change old, limiting beliefs into new, empowering ones. With the Spirit's influence we are able to go with the flow and live in the now moments of life. The Spirit's power helps us show the face of Jesus to the other people on our life bus. We read in Ephesians: "The Spirit is the guarantee that we shall receive what God has promised his people, and this assures us that God will give complete freedom to those who are his" (1:14, GNT).

All you are and all you do—your being and your doing—result from the Holy Spirit's work within you. God is able to do more than you can ask or imagine. As you continue to rely upon this power source and live your Christian beliefs, walking with God becomes a way of life as natural as breathing. But if you don't know you have Holy Spirit power, the joy of the journey will elude you.

There are a few things you can do every day to ensure being connected to the Holy Spirit within, who will lead you to glimpses of God in your life. These simple prescriptives are well within your capabilities, and although they may appear simplistic, they hold incredible power.

## 1. Wake Up Like a Child

Judith Viorst wrote a children's book called *Alexander and the Terrible, Horrible, No Good, Very Bad Day.* The title says it all. Many of us wake up expecting to have a terrible, horrible, no good, very bad day. We create a frame for the day before it even starts. It's like telling yourself, *Here's what the day is going to be like, so deal with it.* At the end of the day, you fall into bed saying, *See, I knew it was going to be a terrible, horrible, no good, very bad day.*

Walking with God starts with your first breath in the morning. Here's simple action to ensure that you're in Holy Spirit mode: wake up with a childlike attitude. Jesus said it so well: "Anyone who will not receive the kingdom of God like a little child will never enter it" (Mark 10:15, NIV).

How did you wake up this morning? Did you think, *Oh no, not another day at the office. Back to the rat race again. I wish it was the weekend?* Did you think, *What a day ahead of me: two meetings, take Timmy to music lessons, go grocery shopping, a dentist appointment, and Bible study tonight?* Did you think, *I wish I could just stay in bed today?*

Imagine waking up like a young child. When a child wakes up, the child doesn't say something like, "Oh darn, I'll have to play with Billy today. I'll probably have to ride my bicycle, and I bet I'm going to have chocolate pudding for dessert again." No, a child wakes up expecting a brand new day with endless possibilities. A child gets out of bed and on the way to a day that is sure to be wonderful.

*A child wakes up expecting a brand new day with endless possibilities. A child gets out of bed and on the way to a day that is sure to be wonderful.*

When you wake up in the morning, take a few moments to see the day as a new beginning. The saying "Today is the first day of the rest of your life" isn't just a trite saying. It's actually profound, and it expresses the essence of a healthy approach to each day.

When I went to camp as a child, the campers all gathered around the flagpole to start our day. Every morning, someone read "Salute to the Dawn":

> So here hath been dawning
> > Another blue day:
> Think, wilt thou let it
> > Slip useless away ?
>
> Out of Eternity
> > This new day is born;
> Into Eternity
> > At night will return.
>
> Behold it aforetime
> > No eye ever did;
> So soon it forever
> > From all eyes is hid.
>
> Here hath been dawning
> > Another blue day:
> Think, wilt thou let it
> > Slip useless away?—Thomas Carlyle

Joshua 24:15 tells us to "choose for yourselves this day whom you will serve" (NIV). Each morning make a conscious choice to give the day to God. And then let go of the day. It's not your problem anymore. Instead, look forward to its unfolding with childlike eagerness, secure in the knowledge that whatever happens, God is present and able to keep you in the palm of God's hand.

## 2. Stay in Touch

Do you talk to yourself? I do. I find myself carrying on an inner conversation with myself as I go about my tasks—cleaning, shopping, cooking. I argue, complain, rejoice, and plead. Someone once said that talking to yourself is okay as long as you don't start answering back!

I talk to Jesus in the same way. It's an inner dialogue. I suppose it's prayer, but I never really think of it that way. It's just talking to a good friend, someone who really listens, someone who cares. When I see an ambulance, I say, *Please take care of whoever is inside.* When I go on stage for a speaking engagement, I always, say, *Over to you, Lord.* When I'm enjoying a particularly luscious ice cream cone, I say, *Thanks for ice cream.* Not very profound, I know, but the connection is made.

My friend Kris and I used to walk our dogs together every day. We'd head out along the road, the animals pulling at their leashes, and follow the familiar path to the beach. The walks usually lasted about an hour, and in that hour we talked.

When you walk with a friend, there are moments of silence, but usually conversation flows. You talk about important things, mundane things, things that are happening in the world, in your life, in your heart. It's the same on your daily walk with God. There are moments of silence, but conversation is welcome. You share the experience with God, which builds confidence that you are not alone, that a good friend walks with you. Continually opening the communication channel between you and God is vital for your Christian walk.

Perhaps you have old friends whom you don't see very often; yet, when you pick up the telephone—even if months have passed—you feel as though only a day has passed. When my mother died several years ago, I had an obituary published in our hometown paper. I hadn't been back to that city in many years, nor had I kept in touch with anyone there. Shortly afterward, I received an online condolence that had been e-mailed to the funeral home. It was from Dotsie, a childhood friend. We'd lost touch when I went off to college, and now, thirty-five years later, she reached out to me. I wrote back; she wrote back.

*When you stop limiting prayer to special times like Sunday or bedtime, you find prayer becomes part of the daily fabric of living.*

Thirty-five years were as nothing in our relationship. We simply picked up where we had left off when I was a bridesmaid in her wedding. Now, four years later, we e-mail back and forth several times a month. The feelings of friendship are as strong as ever.

It's the same between you and God. You may not have been in touch with God lately. That happens sometimes. But God's waiting. Simply reach out and speak to God again. You will be amazed at how easy it is. The old feeling returns. The relationship still exists.

If you consider this gentle daily communication as prayer, everything changes. When you stop limiting prayer to special times like Sunday or bedtime, you find prayer becomes part of the daily fabric of living. Just as you talk to your family, your friends, your coworkers, the people around you, you now talk to God in the same way. No longer is communication with God reserved for "holy occasions." Instead, every occasion becomes holy.

## 3. Experience the Mystical

We may have mountaintop experiences with God, but they are by nature fleeting and soon forgotten. Like Peter, who saw Jesus transfigured, we may try to cling to those moments, wanting to build a tent in order to prolong or repeat the experience. However, like Peter, we all must come down from the mountain sooner or later.

We can experience that same sense of wonder, awe, and presence of God with us when we are far from the mountain and engrossed in daily living. Our most mystical experiences of God often come when we least expect them. They come in the ordinary days of our lives, but they can lift us to the top of the mountain.

What are these mystical experiences? They are experiences with deep meaning that take you out of your mundane surroundings. They cause a shift to another level of awareness, which allows you to gain perspective on your own small human drama.

*Our most mystical experiences of God often come when we least expect them. They come in the ordinary days of our lives, but they can lift us to the top of the mountain.*

You need to experience wonder regularly, to connect with a sense of awe. You might experience such wonder at the birth of a kitten, the blossoming of a beautiful flower, a glorious sunset, an extraordinary piece of music, a memorable dream, a smile across the room. That special wonder might result from a simple moment of laughter or the euphoria of physical exercise. The source could be amazement at the power of a computer, the breathtaking speed with which e-mail circles the globe, or the instant information available on a computer monitor in front of you. These are the mystical moments in your daily life.

## 4. Remember to Be

In my first book, *The Daisies Are Still Free* (Upper Room, 1982), I quoted the following passage as my starting point:

> If I had my life to live over again, I'd try to make more mistakes next time. I would relax. I would limber up. I would be sillier than I have been this trip. I know of very few things I would take seriously. I would take more trips. I would climb more mountains, swim more rivers, and watch more sunsets. I would do more walking and looking. I would eat more ice cream and less beans. I would have more actual troubles and fewer imaginary ones. You see, I am one of those people who live prophylactically and sensibly and sanely hour after hour, day after day. Oh, I've had my moments and if I had it to do over again, I'd have more of them. In fact I'd try to have nothing else. Just moments, one after another, instead of living so many years ahead each day. I have been one of those people who never go anywhere without a thermometer, a hot water bottle, a gargle, a raincoat, aspirin, and a parachute. If I had it to do over again, I would go places, do things and travel lighter than I have.
>
> If I had my life to live over, I would start barefooted earlier in the spring and stay that way later in the fall. I would play hooky more. I wouldn't make such good grades except by accident. I would ride on more merry-go-rounds. I'd pick more daisies.—Brother Jeremiah *

In the preface of that earlier book, I noted having read the piece two years before and said, "It's taken me all this time to discover that picking the daisies is not simply being a free spirit—free from cares, frustrations, worries, fears. Being a barefooted daisy picker is *being*, just *being*. The freedom is within, not without, and it's there for anyone. If I can find it, you can."

Nearly twenty-five years later, I'm still singing the same song! The essence of living the Christian life to its fullest remains the

* "I'd Pick More Daisies" by Brother Jeremiah originally appeared in *Christian Athlete* (October 1974), publication of the Fellowship of Christian Athletes.

same—*being*. Whether you're being a barefooted daisy picker or being a lily—*being* is all that God requires of you. God will do the rest.

Thoreau said most of us "lead lives of quiet desperation." I think that sums up how most people go through life—with no glimpses of God. God is already in your life—in every moment, every second, every hour; every joy, every fear, every experience. You just don't see God. You've experienced the presence of God before, and you can experience it again and again—right now. More importantly, you can glimpse God at any time. I'm going to repeat that phrase because it is crucial in your faith walk with God. *You can glimpse God at any time.*

To experience the presence of God every day, just remember the four simple daily actions that open you up to glimpses of "God with us." Wake up like a child. Stay in touch. Experience the mystical. Remember to *be*.

## Group Exercises

- Briefly share reflections on the previous chapter's "Things to Do" exercises.
- Sit quietly together for a few moments. What is one thing in this room or in this group that could be described as mystical? Why?

## Questions for Group Discussion or Private Reflection

1. Do you have any Zen windows in your home? How would you describe them?
2. How did you feel when you woke up this morning? How has the day turned out?
3. How would you describe your prayer life? Is it all you want it to be? Why or why not?
4. Where have you experienced the mystical?

5. Read the Brother Jeremiah passage on page 140 again. How do these words make you feel? What would you change about your life if you could start over? Is it too late to make some changes now? Why or why not?

*Worry less. Take time to appreciate*

## Prayer Concerns

Loving God, I thank you for bringing me this far in the journey with you. As I continue with you now, help me to remain close, to feel your loving presence, to be aware of your all-encompassing grace. Teach me how to walk closely with you for the rest of my days. I ask this in the name of your son, my Savior, Jesus Christ. Amen.

## Journal Exercise

Skim through your journal entries. You don't need to read every word on every page, but get a sense of the journey you've been on. Then answer the following questions:

What have I learned from this experience?

What will I do differently from this point on?

What insight has changed the way I walk with God?

Finish by writing the passage Romans 8:38-39 in your journal.

# Two Things to Do

1. Commit yourself to fulfilling the actions you've chosen and recorded in your journal—which may include

   opening up to others
   knocking on doors
   treating yourself as a loved person
   doing tasks with joy and pleasure
   living in the now
   giving your stressors to God
   praying for your fellow passengers
   outflowing anonymously to people
   splashing paint on the barn of your life
   and learning how to lily

   Keep a record of what you do, why you do it, how it feels, and whether it moves you closer to God.

2. Commit yourself to continuing your journal. You don't have to write in it every day, but it's a good idea to set aside a regular time, perhaps once a week, when you can contemplate where you are and where you are going. This practice also gives you the opportunity to determine whether you are remaining close to God. If your journaling suggests you are beginning to feel God is far away, remind yourself, *Stick close to God.* And do something about it.

# About the Author

PATRICIA WILSON has been executive director of her own company, Life Track, for the past twenty years. The company has provided training for both secular and Christian groups, and Patricia has conducted more than one hundred business seminars across Canada and the United States annually. Now retired from the international professional-speaker circuit, she still conducts seminars and workshops for various groups and churches. She devotes most of her time to writing. She is also author of *Quiet Spaces: Prayer Interludes for Women*. Patricia and her husband, Gerald, have three grown children and live in Nova Scotia.